Mary Curran Hackett

HARPERCOLLINS
LEADERSHIP
AN IMPRINT OF HARPERCOLLINS

THE SEPHORA STORY

The Retail Success You Can't Make Up

Published by HarperCollins Leadership, an imprint of HarperCollins Focus LLC.

Published in association with Kevin Anderson & Associates: https://www.ka-writing.com/.

Book design by Aubrey Khan, Neuwirth & Associates.

ISBN 978-1-4002-2059-5 (eBook)
ISBN 978-1-4002-2058-8 (HC)

Library of Congress Control Number: 2020931344

20 21 22 23 LSC 10 9 8 7 6 5 4 3 2 1

CONTENTS

AUTHOR'S NOTE

Sephora did not respond to requests for interviews. All interviews and quotes come directly from online presentations, news articles, books, case studies, as well as Sephora's website and press releases.

"We aim to be the best-loved and most-admired beauty community in the world."

—CHRISTOPHER DE LAPUENTE,
CEO, Sephora

1969

Dominique Mandonnaud opens a small boutique perfume shop in Limoges, France.

1970

Boots PLC in the United Kingdom also opens its first perfume store in Paris.

1976

Boots and Nouvelles Galeries form a partnership to build Sephora perfume chain.

1979

Mandonnaud launches Shop 8 with an "assisted self-service" retail perfume format.

1984

Promodès acquires control of Shop 8.

1988

Shop 8 acquires eight perfume stores in Paris.

1993

Shop 8 launches its new Mille et un Parfums retail format, then acquires the Sephora chain from Boots, rebranding all its stores.

1991

Mandonnaud, backed by two equity investment firms, buys out Shop 8.

1996

Sephora opens its flagship store on the Champs-Élysées in Paris.

1997

Mandonnaud and investors sell Sephora to LVMH Moët Hennessy Louis Vuitton SA; Sephora acquires the Marie Jeanne-Godard perfume chain.

Sephora faces a series of alleged
discrimination incidents and launches its
"We Belong to Something Beautiful" campaign
under new CEO Jean-André Rougeot.

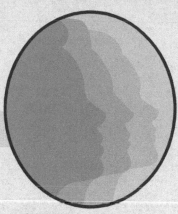

2018

Fast Company names Sephora
to their top fifty list of
"World's Most Innovative Companies."

2017

Sephora opens in New York City's
Herald Square, becoming the largest of
Sephora's North American stores and
one of six TIP Workshop locations,
with interactive services and tools.

2014

Calvin McDonald replaces
David Suliteanu as president
and CEO of Sephora Americas.

2007

Sephora opens to the Middle Eastern
markets and opens over 44 Sephora UAE and
KSA stores as well as online.

2004

Sephora debuts
in Canada.

2003

Jacques Levy is appointed CEO and leads
the redevelopment of the Sephora format.

1999

Sephora launches online.

1998

Sephora opens its first store in
New York City, launching an
international expansion drive.

"Never underestimate any woman's desire for beauty."

—ESTÉE LAUDER

INTRODUCTION

Very few industries and retailers these days can say they are "Amazon-proof" or even "Recession-proof." That is unless you're in the global cosmetics business, which is expected to grow 7 percent a year over the next three years—reaching 806 billion dollars by 2023, according to Orbis Research.[1] Companies like Sephora, and its competitors, Ulta, Dermstore, Nordstrom, and Macy's, are no exception. In fact, since its founding in 1969 by Dominique Mandonnaud, Sephora has grown from a small perfume shop in Paris to one of the leading beauty product retailers in the world. Beauty product retailers like them, which carry cosmetics, skin care, body care, fragrance, nail color, beauty supplements, styling and beauty tools seem to be impervious to the ebbs and flows of the economy. When other industries and companies have floundered to stay afloat, Sephora has adapted, innovated, and risen above.

Some argue the reason the beauty industry, as a whole, is thriving is because of all the rampant societal pressure and norms that increasingly suggest that *younger is better*. Globally we are seeing an increased aging population[2] who simply can't abide wrinkles, dry skin, blotchy skin tones, freckles, age spots, adult acne, thinning brows, upper lip fuzz, broken, damaged, or graying hair, or any other unseemly looks on the "beauty don't lists." It's not just the aging populations that are feeling the heat and raising the demand for more advanced beauty products. With the widespread use of social media—YouTube, Facebook, Instagram, Twitter, Snapchat, and TikTok—it's nearly impossible for young people to escape the social pressure to appear beautiful at all times. Some critics even go so far as to blame the cosmetic and beauty industries for raising the standards of beauty in order to market and prey on an unsuspecting public. While the beauty industry isn't completely blameless, it's not solely responsible either. The desire to be young and beautiful dates further back than the inception of Instagram, or even the makeup counter, for that fact. Companies like Sephora have found success not because they have marketed or preyed upon the insecurities of individuals, but rather they have anticipated their deepest needs, desires, and hopes and responded in kind. Well aware that feeling beautiful is more than skin deep and is an intrinsic desire, Sephora meets its customers where there are.

> Companies like Sephora have found success not because they have marketed or preyed upon the insecurities of individuals, but rather they have anticipated their deepest needs, desires, and hopes and responded in kind.

In fact, the name *Sephora* harkens back to beauty's historical (or more accurately literary and etymological) origins. Sephora is a mashup of *sephos,* which means beauty in Greek, and *Zipporah,* which was the name of the Biblical Moses's beautiful wife, whose name in Greek is spelled *Sepphora.*

The desire to be look and *feel* beautiful and youthful is not something Madison Avenue advertising agencies and cosmetic companies invented. Long before Insta influencers were trying on mascara and making serum recs, in prehistoric times red ochre was used as a way to decorate the skin (and discovered in excavated graves of our female genetic ancestors) and over a thousand years ago women and men painted their eyes with kohl, sprayed perfume, used red rouge lipstick,[3] and soaked in warm baths of milk and honey. The desire to luxuriate, accentuate one's most beautiful features, satisfy the senses, or even change one's look has been a driving force in humanity for eons.

A Very Brief History of Makeup: "I Am Ready for My Close-up, Mr. DeMille"

Though the desire to be beautiful may be as old as civilization itself, Teresa Riordan's 2004 book, *Inventing Beauty,* argues that as photography became more popular and widespread (somewhere after 1870) cosmetics did as well. Prior to this, makeup was reserved for the tawdrier members of society, i.e. the euphemistically called "Ladies of the night," and of course, thespians whose faces needed to stand out under the harsh lighting and seen from the back of theatre. But with the rise of photography and cinema, cosmetics became mainstream. As early as the 1880s, many budding entrepreneurs saw the opportunity to create cosmetics so their customers could look as beautiful as the women in the magazines and advertising. Most of these companies were independently owned and operated by women—the most popular being the California Perfume Company, which later became Avon. Individual agents—mostly women—sold beautifying creams, lotions, and facial tints to their friends and family members. This unique business model allowed women to become more financially independent. It also meant that with more women working in the cosmetics industry there was more money to spend on cosmetics. It's a win-win formula that still is winning today for similar tier-marketing cosmetic companies like Mary Kay, Arbonne, and Beautycounter, which afford women the opportunity to earn money as entrepreneurs, cosmetic agents, and makeup artists.[4]

 As early as the 1880s, many budding entrepreneurs saw the opportunity to create cosmetics so their customers could look as beautiful as the women in the magazines and advertising. Most of these companies were independently owned and operated by women—the most popular being the California Perfume Company, which later became Avon.

Even during serious economic downturns, cosmetic sales steadily increased.[5] Where other industries completely collapsed, makeup was a simple, small luxury a woman could afford in desperate times. Instead of rationalizing buying a dress or a pair of shoes to feel pretty, a woman could simply purchase an inexpensive tube of lipstick and feel instantly glamorous.

Modern Cosmetics and the Beauty Industry

By the early 1900s, however, makeup had become a mainstay, not to mention part of the lexicon. Perhaps the most notable makeup artist of this era and the founding father of the modern cosmetics industry is Max Factor. In the early 1900s, he was a famed wigmaker and face artist for Hollywood studios and he developed a "greasepaint" foundation that didn't crack or flake off.[6] It was an instant sensation. It wasn't long before actresses began wearing it offscreen as well. Factor went on to develop lip gloss and eyebrow pencils, and "pan-cake" compact of powdered foundation called "Pan-Cake Brand Make Up." Many attribute the term *makeup* (now just one word) to him because of this. It's considered the first time the term is seen or used in media advertising. By the 1920s, he took his products to the mass market with a promise to his female customers that they too could look like movie stars. Ad copy along with featured stars like Judy Garland, Rita Hayworth, Lana Turner, Merle Oberon, and Ella Raines, promised "This is make-up that actually creates glamour . . . . The Screen Star Secret that beautifies instantly." Who wouldn't want to look like Rita Hayworth or Lana Turner?

Max Factor hit pay dirt. But, he wasn't the only one.

Around the same time in 1915, T.L. Williams started Maybelline Company, though at first it was only an eye-makeup company. In truth, the makeup was his sister Mabel's idea, or rather a result of her resourcefulness. After singeing her lashes off by accident, she mixed coal dust and Vaseline and applied to what was left of her lashes to duplicate the look of real ones. She discovered she could make them look even longer, replicating the look of the big-eyed Hollywood starlets like Mary Pickford. A savvy businessman, her brother packaged the concoctions (without actual coal) in a tin and called it Lash-Brow-Ine. He named the brand itself Maybelline by combining *Mabel* and *Vaseline*.[7] Our idea of what constitutes an acceptable lash length has never been the same since. Thanks, Mabel.

For the first part of the twentieth century the makeup industry grew as the proliferation of women's magazines (which required ads for makeup and other popular items for women) also flourished. However, the *way* in which customers purchased and experienced makeup began to change by the end of World War II. Prior to this time period most makeup was typically available by mail order, behind the counter at department stores, or through independent agents. But thanks in large part to Estée Lauder, founder of the eponymous brand of makeup that still exists today, the cosmetic buying experience fundamentally changed. In 1946, Lauder began what was to become a massive makeup empire though a particularly revolutionary approach— by meeting women where they were. Or should we say, where they would be a captive audience to hearing about skincare. *Where was that?* At beauty salons of course. With women stuck under hair dryers, she gave away free samples as well as bonus gifts of the skin cream that she developed with her uncle. In addition to her unique marketing and sales approach, she allowed customers to interact with her products. Eventually Saks Fifth Avenue placed an order, and it was there that she continued to give away free samples, added gifts, and focused on recurring personalized marketing techniques to build brand loyalty.[8] Her approach proved successful. Since launching the Estée Lauder brand in 1946, the Lauder family has expanded to include a number of popular brands as well, including but not limited to Bobbi Brown, Clinique, Origins, Glamglow, Prescriptives, La Mer, MAC, Smashbox, Too Faced, Aerin, Becca, haircare lines Aveda and Bumble and Bumble, and numerous fragrance lines. In many ways Lauder was the pioneer of the modern cosmetics industry, and paved the ways for stores like Sephora, which not only carry most of her brands today but also meets the customer where they are (not in beauty salons, but rather online, in store, on social media), offer free samples and free gifts with purchase, showcase interactive displays, as well as provide recurring personalized marketing and brand loyalty programs.

> **In 1946, Lauder began what was to become a massive makeup empire though a particularly revolutionary approach— by meeting women where they were. Or should we say, where they would be a captive audience to hearing about skincare. *Where was that?* At beauty salons of course.**

The modern cosmetics and beauty industry (and thankfully the science behind it) has come a long way, and not just from the days of Cleopatra's Egypt, but from Max Factor's "grease-paint" and "pan-cake" makeup tins as well. Gone are the days

of painting one's face with poisonous ceruse and other hazard-
ous lead- and arsenic-based methods. In addition to scientific
and technological advances in the past 150 years, the entire
beauty industry has grown exponentially and become an inte-
gral part of the growing global economy.

Sephora's Origin Story Linked to the Past

Sephora has been one of those companies leading the way for
the past fifty years. They've been doing so both differently and
better than their competitors thanks in part to their strategy,
which Dominique Mandonnaud introduced when he opened
his small perfume shop in Limoges, France, in 1969. Perhaps
inspired by Estée Lauder's approach, or perhaps his own need
and desire to interact with the product, Mandonnaud wanted
to create an experiential encounter. Where he lived, most
women and men shopping for perfumes were separated from
the products by a counter, which was managed by a sales asso-
ciate. There was very little experiential nature to the purchase.
He wanted to interact with products when he shopped, and
thought customers would want to too. He didn't just want to
sell a product—he wanted to provide an experience. *Come in,
walk up to the perfume, hold it in your hands, spray it on your own
wrists, and savor it—maybe go home with a sample to try out for a day
or two.* Though in 1969 there was no data to show, as there is
today, just how compelling and effective this experience actually was in order to close a sale, Mandonnaud knew intuitively
that this was where the beauty industry needed to go.

Much like Lauder, Mandonnaud believed the future of
beauty meant removing the barriers between the customer and
the product—and it meant meeting the customer where they

were. Like Max Factor, Mandonnaud believed his customers should feel extremely special, as if they were walking onto a theatrical stage and playing the starring role in their own lives. In fact, up until 2018, the sales floor in Sephora was called *the stage*, and all the employees were referred to as *stage directors*, their black and red (now just black and white) uniforms were called *costumes*, the back area of the store was called *backstage*, and the customers were referred to as, you guessed it, *cast members*. Like Mabel Williams, Mandonnaud was resourceful and innovative, always looking for the newest and best ways to please and delight his customers. Though a lot has changed in the past few years for the cosmetic industry, especially with the rise of the digital age, Sephora hasn't loosened its foothold on the experiential component its stores offer.

> " Perhaps inspired by Estée Lauder's approach, or perhaps his own need and desire to interact with the product, Mandonnaud wanted to create an experiential encounter.

What to Expect in This Book

In this book you will find out how Mandonnaud transformed a small perfume boutique into an international beauty retailer. You will learn how he and then his business partners and subsequent CEOs overcame obstacles all along the way. You'll also learn the strategies and practices they employed through the years to adapt to the fast-paced and competitive beauty industry. You'll learn how Sephora was on the vanguard of the beauty industry's role in the digital marketplace, and how they used innovative test-and-learn practices, high-tech tools, as well as data to transform the cosmetic and skincare buying experience. Finally, you'll find out how they dealt with pitfalls and major challenges, like lawsuits, scandals, diversity and inclusion issues, and how they plan to meet the ever-changing and evolving retail landscape in the future.

Ultimately, you will learn how Sephora has evolved and adapted to the digital age with a proven business model that is the envy not just of the cosmetics world, but of all retail. Sephora's unique strategy relies on data and technology to fully understand their customers' needs. Over the years, Sephora's commitment to cast members'—ahem, *customers'*—satisfaction has driven them to pioneer and create tech-enabled retail experiences. Like many innovative companies that rely on data and innovation—through test and learn iterations—Sephora is no exception. They continuously exceed the expectations of their customers and have held their own against massive competition—big box retailers, apparel retailers, department stores, niche clean beauty retailers, direct marketing retailers, online retailers, and even the great retail annihilator, Amazon.

Sephora is now the world's leading specialist perfume retailer, with over 2,600 stores in thirty-four countries.[9] They are also a beauty/cosmetic brand in their own right and have developed their own private, affordably priced label, Sephora Collection brand cosmetics, as well as the world-renowned anti-wrinkle and skincare product, StriVectin-SD. In addition to being a retailer, cosmetic brand, and skincare line, they have also expanded their services to offer in-store services, classes, and events, as well as provide fully interactive online communities as well. Now the subsidiary of luxury goods group LVMH Moët Hennessy Louis Vuitton S.A., which owns many of the brands positioned on Sephora's shelves, Sephora is the largest unit of LVMH's Selective Retailing Division, and has exceeded revenues of six billion dollars and has no plans to slow down anytime soon.

❝ Sephora is now the world's leading specialist perfume retailer, with over 2,600 stores in thirty-four countries.

"Consumers are looking for retail stores to be creative spaces. They are looking for experiences."

—BRIDGET DOLAN,
SVP OMNI Experience & Innovation, Sephora

CHAPTER ONE

THE EARLY YEARS

When Dominique Mandonnaud opened his small single perfume store in Limoges, France, it was nearly impossible for a customer to get up close and personal with the product. Up until then, the French perfume and cosmetics market relied on a commission- and service-based retail model. In other words, the sales staff received a percentage of each product sold. They typically operated out of department stores, where each sales person was assigned one particular brand. Though the self-service model was pervasive in grocery stores and pharmacies by then, high-end perfume and cosmetics required a sales person. Mandonnaud hoped to change all that.

By 1979, he changed his perfume shop's name to Shop 8, and he reconfigured and designed it so that there was a large open selling floor, and products were all within reach of the customers. He also expanded his product offerings from perfume to include cosmetics as well. What was truly innovative was that rather than dividing products up by brand, he divided by product. In other words, if you needed a night cream, you would go to the night cream section and see Elizabeth Arden's night cream next to Estée Lauder's and Chanel's. Customers could compare products and make their own decision on what was best for them. It was a wholly revolutionary approach to selling cosmetics and perfume—and his customers loved it. Over the next several years, Mandonnaud honed and perfected the Shop 8 "assisted self-service" format, while expanding his organization. By 1984, Mandonnaud had four Shop 8 stores.

Later that same year, the distribution group Promodès, which was looking to expand, purchased Mandonnaud's Shop 8. Though there are no details anywhere in the public domain about what happened, the relationship, according to the history of Sephora on Cenage's Encyclopedia.com website was said to have "soured."[1] Interestingly enough, when searching for Dominque Mandonnaud's version of the story there is virtually zero digital footprint, which makes a person wonder: what are they trying to cover up? Wild conspiracy theories aside, we'll stick to the facts: There are no interviews, no reports, or detailed articles explaining the separation. All that is known, according to this one source, is that in 1987 "Promodès had separated itself from Shop 8."[2]

> " Interestingly enough, when searching for Dominque Mandonnaud's version of the story there is virtually zero digital footprint, which makes a person wonder: what are they trying to cover up?

However, at some point while working with Promodès, Mandonnaud borrowed capital from them to expand. This meant that when Promodès separated from Shop 8, Mandonnaud still owed Promodès a considerable amount, so much so that Promodès was still considered to have the majority of voting rights. This proved to be quite the impediment for Mandonnaud. Mandonnaud hoped to expand in Paris. If he was going to sell perfumes and cosmetics, the best market to do that was in the fashion and perfume capital of the world. He hoped to purchase a chain of eight Parisian perfume stores, and hoped to convert them into his Shop 8 format. However, citing his debts, Promodès denied Mandonnaud the necessary funds to infuse the perfume chain.

Upset by this refusal but not undeterred, Mandonnaud hoped to simply buy back his shares of the company to regain full control. Promodès, however, set a high asking price for the company. Though we don't know what the price was, we do know that Mandonnaud didn't have the capital to buy back his Shop 8 because he reached out to a private equity firm, Apax Partners. He also reached out to another private equity group, Astorg. By getting backing of two private equity firms together, Mandonnaud was finally able to buy out Promodès. In addition to helping him buy out the chain, the two equity firms were in full agreement with Mandonnaud's plan to expand the company. They also approved Mandonnaud's conditions for their own exit: All would exit the agreement, including Mandonnaud, on Mandonnaud's fiftieth birthday, September 5, 1997, the date which he planned on retiring.

How Shop 8 Became Sephora

By 1991, the buyout was complete and on paper Apax was the majority stakeholder, but it seemed more like an equitable partnership. Though Apax held the majority of the shares, it was in full support of Mandonnaud's plan to expand his company from three to five stores per year.

However, once again Mandonnaud was met with another unforeseen obstacle—the recession of 1991. It wasn't just France that was feeling the economic pinch; The entire global economy was shrinking.[3] Not exactly the time, one would think, to expand a luxury item goods chain.

However, before the word *pivot* was shouted by Ross on *Friends* or used ad nauseum by entrepreneurs and startups to describe quick about-faces in strategy, Mandonnaud and his partners pivoted. Instead of expanding their own line of stores by three or four stores at a time, they thought to take advantage of the economic downturn, specifically the lower valuations of companies, and purchased an already existing perfume chain in order to expand.

Meanwhile, Mandonnaud hadn't forgotten about his own stores. Still committed to his vision of creating what he dubbed "assisted self-service" stores, where customers could interact with products while still asking for help if need be, Mandonnaud launched a new store called, Mille et un Parfums in the Belle-Épine shopping mall in Val-de-Marne (near Paris). In addition to the "assisted self-service" model, he established a large selling space that was more upscale than mall-like or even pharmacy-like—relying on luxurious details like backlit display cases and refined graphic design elements throughout the store.

This Is Where It Gets Complicated

Not all companies' stories are linear or even straightforward. While it's easy to say Dominique Mandonnaud "founded" Sephora, it's not entirely true. What he founded was the company that ultimately bought *Sephora*. Say what now?

> " Not all companies' stories are linear or even straightforward. While it's easy to say Dominique Mandonnaud "founded" Sephora, it's not entirely true. What he founded was the company that ultimately bought *Sephora*.

Let's back up. Sephora was actually the name of a company of chain stores owned and operated by the United Kingdom's Boots PLC. Boots, the parent company, was founded by John Boots in 1849 as an herbal medicine shop and expanded over the years to be a full-service pharmaceutical company. In fact, in the 1960s, Boots chemists John Nicholson and Stewart Adams developed ibuprofen in its labs. (A moment of silence for these intrepid heroes: All hail ibuprofen.) Over the years through several different transactions it became The Boots Pure Drug Company, and eventually, in 1971, The Boots Company Limited. Over the past 165 years they have expanded their market from drugs and remedies to pharmacies, opticians, dentistry, cosmetics, beauty supplies and what they call "well-being services."[4]

During one of their expansion periods they purchased a chain of cosmetic stores, which *they* named Sephora in 1970. There is absolutely no mention of it on the Boots website and there is no history of an owner of this chain prior to 1970. (Interesting to note: When reading about the history of Sephora, depending on which website you happen to be perusing, some say the company was founded in 1969 and others say 1970.) If you're a Francophile, chances are you're going with the 1969 timeline. It was, after all, Mandonnaud's idea to purchase the Sephora chain, and it was his unique approach to the cosmetic retail experience that made the company what it is today. But if you're an Anglophile, chances are you're going with 1970 as the founding date, when the UK Boots bought the chain and named it Sephora. Sephora, the company today, plays the part of Switzerland here. They split the difference, citing on their website's About Us page, "Sephora was found in France by Dominique Mandonnaud" (nod to France and Mandonnaud) "in 1970" (nod to Boots and the UK). From one writer to another: As Bridget Jones would say, *Well done you, Sephora copywriter.*

In 1993, Shop 8 (Mandonnaud) through his investor, purchased Sephora from Boots for the equivalent of sixty-one million dollars. At the time, Boots PLC owned a total of thirty-eight Sephora-branded chain stores in the Paris area, the oldest one being the one on Paris's Rue de Passy, which opened in 1970. During this time Sephora was the largest perfume specialist in France. The Sephora chains under Boots control in France ran their stores like they did in their Boots UK stores. There were both high-end luxury items alongside mass market goods.

This acquisition ultimately expanded Shop 8's total network to nearly fifty stores. It also gave Shop 8 prime locations. Sephora was already in popular Parisian shopping areas and had an established brand recognition. Immediately after the purchase, Mandonnaud made a major two-fold announcement. First, he intended for all of his new stores to follow his Mille et un Parfums' format—assisted self-service with a focus on luxurious details in a wide open selling floor plan. Second, all of his stores, including Shop 8, would now be rebranded as Sephora.

Over the next four years, Mandonnaud continued to expand. By 1997—his fiftieth year and intended retirement date—Mandonnaud operated fifty-four stores throughout all of France. Sephora also controlled 8 percent of the total French perfume market.[5] In some ways, Sephora was making its name as somewhat of a travel destination. People from all over the world flocked to his famed flagship store on Champs-Élysées in Paris. It was there the iconic black and white stripes, reminiscent of Siena Cathedral's black-and-white striped façade, first appeared.

> **By 1997—his fiftieth year and intended retirement date—Mandonnaud operated fifty-four stores throughout all of France.**

Today, no matter where you are, what mall you're in, what country you happen to find yourself in, you'll see the faux stone black and white horizontal stripes as a beacon, luring you in to try just one shade of lipstick, one serum (okay, maybe seven, but who's counting). The store on Champs-Élysées was three-times the average store size, roughly, thirteen hundred square meters and was the template for all future stores. Mandonnaud had finally seen his dream incarnate—from a small boutique in Limogoes to the preeminent shopping avenue in Paris. Mandonnaud had plenty of reason to both celebrate and even, stick around. It was clear, Sephora was here to stay.

Mandonnaud's Retirement and a New Parent Company

However, Mandonnaud was very clear about creating his company with the end—particularly his own role—in mind. He knew his company would grow and succeed, even without him, and so as originally planned he set out to retire in 1997. His partners, too, were fully prepared to exit their investments as well, as stipulated in their original agreement. Instead of opting for a public offering, Mandonnaud and his partners began looking for interested (and worthy) buyers. There was a none more worthy luxury beauty retailer than LVMH. Coincidentally, LVMH was also actively looking for ways to expand, especially by adding a retail component to complement their designer label products. With time to spare (two months' shy of his September birthday), Mandonnaud sold his beloved company to LVMH in July 1997 for 344 million dollars—thus making Mandonnaud and his two investors a handsome profit. Quite the fiftieth birthday present for Mandonnaud. It was also the dawn of a new era for Sephora.

Sephora Becomes Part of LVMH

Once part of the LVMH family, Sephora was infused with available capital and was able to expand even further. In 1998, it doubled its existing number of stores after it acquired French perfume chain, Marie Jeanne-Godard.[6] All seventy-five of its stores were rebranded under the Sephora name, and the purchase quickly resulted in added revenue. It also meant that now Sephora controlled 18 percent of the French perfume market. And within a year of being owned by LVMH, Sephora's sales reached FRF two billion.[7] Sephora was ready to expand beyond France. It was ready to go global.

"People like the entertainment environment. It's the wave of the future."

—ANNETTE GREEN,
president of the Fragrance Foundation

CHAPTER TWO

FROM BOUTIQUE TO A BEAUTY EMPIRE

"This is a beauty junkie's paradise," exclaimed then co-host for ABC's *The View*, Lisa Ling, during the 1998 grand opening event for Sephora's first flagship in the US.[1] In her article "Looks Matter" for *People*, writer Julie K.L. Dam was an invited guest to the grand opening event and reported on celebrity guests' reactions to the massive cosmetics store. Actress Kyra Sedgwick was on hand for the opening too, and faced with the overwhelming store carrying over 600 fragrances and 365 shades of lipstick, said to Dam, "That's a little scary, but I'm up for the challenge."[2]

In the same article, Sephora's then artistic director, Chafik, (he dropped his last name Gasmi), told Dam what he felt the purpose of Sephora's store layout is: "When you come here, the place is enticing and a delight to the senses."[3] Dam, for her part, shared her own insights after experiencing the store for the first time, "Make that an assault on the senses: Sephora's dizzying collection of 300 different brands from Hard Candy to Christian

Dior, plus its own line, makes it the Barnes & Noble of beauty retailers. Instead of hiding the goodies behind the counter as most competitors do, Sephora puts everything on open display, tempting customers to spritz, paint, and blend at will."[4] Granted, the Barnes & Noble analogy doesn't hold up with time, but for those of us who remember spending hours sipping coffee, pouring over magazines and sampling books before buying them at seemingly ubiquitous Barnes & Noble shops around the country, the analogy makes sense. Up until Sephora, the best we cosmetic shoppers could do was loiter in the CVS or Duane Reade aisles, flip packages over, read about them, or hold up shades of lipsticks to our face and take our best guess. Or we could go to a department store and pick one brand, say Clinique, and communicate with a Clinique agent for that brand and that brand alone. Being able to sample makeup and cosmetics of innumerable brands side by side without an independent selling agent was indeed revolutionary. It was also great fun.

> " Make that an assault on the senses: Sephora's dizzying collection of 300 different brands from Hard Candy to Christian Dior, plus its own line, makes it the Barnes & Noble of beauty retailers. Instead of hiding the goodies behind the counter as most competitors do, Sephora puts everything on open display, tempting customers to spritz, paint, and blend at will."

In a prescient statement, Annette Green, president of the Fragrance Foundation, not affiliated with Sephora, said at the time, "People like the entertainment environment. It's the wave of the future."[5] Sephora was betting on it. By 1998, Sephora was operating 182 stores in Europe and in the process of opening some thirty-nine stores in the US (in addition to the New York store), and had plans to expand to more than 175 more by 2002. But expansion didn't come without its ups and downs, lawsuits, or even the unique vision and bold moves.

Imitation Is the Sincerest Form of Flattery—And the Quickest Way to Infringe on Trade Dress

Sephora's entrance in the US began to not just shake up the competition, but it got them positively shook. So shook in fact, they started to copy Sephora down to the finest details. Shortly after Sephora launched in New York, it opened its second US store in San Francisco on Stockton Street. Soon after, Macy's redesigned its cosmetic department to look very similar to Sephora's exterior and layout in both their New York's Herald Square store and their Souson, a stand-alone cosmetic and fragrance boutique, in the Santa Clara Valley Mall. Sephora took this seriously and filed a lawsuit on August 11, 1999, stating that "Macy's was infringing on its 'trade dress,' or creating a look and design similar enough to cause customer confusion."[6]

By February 2000, the US District Court granted Sephora's motion for a preliminary injunction, which barred Federated Department Stores, Inc., (Macy's parent company) and its Macy's West division from opening any stand-alone stores or renovating any existing cosmetic departments until the case was resolved.[7] "The plaintiff (Sephora's) shops have a distinctive feel that is closely mimicked by the Macy's facilities," noted Judge R. Walker, according to a Sephora release.[8] The judge agreed with Sephora that indeed, if a customer were to visit a Souson store or the newly renovated Macy's cosmetics departments, he or she would be confused into thinking they entered a store that one would think could be owned or operated by Sephora. According to the law, "Customer confusion is a key element to proving trade dress infringement."[9] The case was set for trial for September 2000, but by June of the same year, Sephora settled its lawsuit with Federated Department Stores Inc. and Macy's West subsidiary. However, the terms of the settlement were never disclosed.[10] While Macy's does still have an "open sell" concept now in its stores, there are clear design differentiators.

The Importance of the Look: Chafik's Lasting Influence

There is something to be said about the fact that a major retailer with a massive foothold in the American retail market like Macy's allegedly started to copy Sephora's design and marketing elements. Sephora was well aware that competition was fierce, and they always had to be a step ahead. Howard Meitner, the CEO and USA president of Sephora at the time of the lawsuit, said competitors/imitators just "put a premium on someone like Chafik, who has the ability to keep us current, keep us ahead." Chafik, as mentioned earlier, was Sephora's artistic director, and was in charge of all of Sephora's aesthetic details, "from the novel circular fragrance-testing stations to the mix of world music that plays in the stores."[11] In Meitner's own words, "someone like Chafik" was incredibly valuable to the entire growth of the brand, and one could argue his unique vision and execution of the brand throughout the world is one of the main reasons for Sephora's success today, if not the reason for its enduring iconic image.

> **Chafik was incredibly valuable to the growth of the brand, and one could argue his unique vision and execution of the brand throughout the world is one of the main reasons for Sephora's success today, if not the reason for its enduring iconic image.**

Chafik could have an entire book written about his incredible life. He's a French-registered architect and industrial designer who found fame in 1997 when he received the *Prix de Nombre d'Or*, a prestigious award for industry and design for his work reinventing the *Moulin Galland* catalogue and creating the "Square" chair which is found in many public places including Times Square and parks the world over. But before his work was internationally recognized, Chafik's unique creative vision caught the eye of Mandonnaud, who tasked him with designing his famed Champs-Élysées store in 1996 and offered him the artistic direction of the brand and the concept. Chafik stayed on with Sephora for seven years, and was responsible for the artistic design of all the international expansion within that time.[12]

After Mandonnaud sold the company to LVMH, Bernard Arnault, the chairman and CEO of LVMH, also requested that Chafik help with his other brands, including Dior, Galliano, Kenzo, Dom Perignon, Guerlain, Givenchy, and Ebel, in order to challenge "all their creative and strategic approaches."[13] Indeed, challenge is something Chafik did well. In a rare interview, Mandonnaud joked to a reporter about Chafik, "He's unbearable! He's a pain! Once he gets hold of an idea he won't let go."[14] One of those ideas was creating a unique sensory experience that entices the buyer through what he calls, "a concept of seduction" no matter where they are anywhere in the world.[15]

Going Global—
Scaling Successes and Snags

While meeting challenges and successes head on in the US, Sephora set its sights on the European market. One of their first forays into the European market was Italy. Sephora began making strategic purchases, including a number of smaller chains, Kharys in 1998, the forty-six-store Laguna chain in 1999, and Boidi, a chain of nineteen perfume stores in 2000.[16] By 2005, Sephora operated more than one hundred stores in Italy, including its Milan flagship location, which opened that same year. While expanding in France, Canada, the US, Italy, Portugal, and Greece, amassing nearly 460 new stores worldwide, all didn't go as smoothly as Armani foundation gliding over Smashbox primer for Sephora. In fact, they were met with considerable clumps in the foundation and more than a few wrinkles, most notably when trying to expand in both the United Kingdom, Japan, and Spain.[17] In Japan, they were met with "relative indifference," and their seven stores were lagging in sales. They had a handful of stores open throughout the UK, which ultimately closed.

> **"** While expanding in France, Canada, the US, Italy, Portugal, and Greece, amassing nearly 460 new stores worldwide, all didn't go as smoothly as Armani foundation gliding over Smashbox primer for Sephora.

Usually dips like this in a brand's performance gets investors talking. Would LVMH sell off what appeared to be a company in crisis? However, it appears as though, despite the mediocre sales, LVMH had no plans of selling off Sephora, rather they hired a new leader. In 2003, after sales had been steadily declining and Sephora struggled to gain ground in places like Spain, Sephora hired former Staples International head, Jacques Levy to lead Sephora as president. Together with European managing director, Nathalie Bader-Michel, Levy initiated what amounted to a total overhauling of the Sephora concept.

Prior to leading Staples, Levy held a series of positions in the distribution sector, working with Darty, Galeries Lafayette/ Nouvelles Galeries and Disney Groups, where he led as the director of operations for Europe and then served as the VP and general manager Global franchise with the Disney Stores. As the president of Staples International for three years, he led during a period of increased profits and expansion, and was poised to do the same for Sephora. Pierre Letzelter, who was the chairman of the Sephora Group at the time said, "We are very pleased to welcome Jacques Levy at the head of Sephora Europe. His international experience and thorough knowledge of distribution, combined with the solid competencies of the teams currently in charge of our different operation, will be great assets to the development of the Sephora concept."[18]

Letzelter's projections proved true. The Levy era, which lasted for seven years, was an era of massive growth, expansion, and profitability.

The Beginning of the Levy Era and Launch of Sephora Collection and StriVectin-SD

One of Levy's most significant contributions was the introduction of the Sephora brand line of its private label cosmetic brand, the Sephora Collection. It was high-end, but low cost, and thought to be innovative and even groundbreaking—creating makeup for the body, not just the face. The tagline for the product today is right on brand with Sephora's super casual, super down-to-earth fresh content: "Yes-way quality for a way-nice price." According to their own website it's for "everyone from rookies to beauty vloggers." The belief behind creating the product line is, according to Sephora's website, "As Sephora's own brand, we flex our extensive industry knowledge to create paycheck-friendly products that perform on par with more spendy ones. So whether you're looking for a ride-or-die eyeliner or a clean skincare routine that doesn't require a small investment, rest assured: Sephora Collection will wow you and your wallet." The website goes on to say that all of Sephora Collection products "comply with the most rigorous international laws on product safety—meaning they satisfy European and US cosmetics regulations. They also satisfy the strictest internal requirements of development, traceability, and safety, and lead by example with a Restricted Substance List that excludes more than 1,400 substances."[19]

In that same year, the beauty world lost its collective mind over what was to become a huge international bestselling anti-aging wrinkle cream, StriVectin-SD, which was developed by Klein-Becker for Sephora. Designed to be a cream to eliminate stretch marks, it quickly was adapted by consumers to combat facial wrinkles and sagging. Within a very short period, it quickly became one of the top sellers in US department stores, online, and specialty stores in the prestige skincare industry. In Sephora's own press release, dated July 19, 2004, just a year after its official launch, it stated, "Move over Botox, women are embracing StriVectin-SD."[20] Citing a study "Beyond Botox: Understanding the StriVectin-SD Consumer," by marketing information company The NPD Group, Sephora reported that StriVectin-SD had achieved over thirteen million dollars in department store sales between May and December of 2003 alone, and by the first months of 2004, it had already generated thirty million dollars. For comparison, that is at a rate of three times the average successful skincare line—which can average between twenty to thirty million dollars in a year.

NPD attributed StriVectin-SD's success to overall customer satisfaction. Results talk, and so do the people who are happy with them. *Ohmygosh, have you had work done? What have you been doing?* are irresistible questions for any person to answer, and yet it was one many were quick to do. Word of mouth seemed to be primarily responsible for the massive success because from a marketing and awareness perspective, StriVectin-SD was a largely unheard of by the mainstream. Despite its huge success, fewer than 5 percent of women were aware of the product and only 12 percent of those owned it. The study was conducted via the internet and was, according to NPD, "geographically and demographically balanced" though not gender balanced, having surveyed 45,000 women. But all that changed soon after the report was released in 2004. StriVectin-SD became the talk of beauty magazines, vloggers, and bloggers, and had consumers begging for more.

> " The beauty world lost its collective mind over what was to become a huge international bestselling anti-aging wrinkle cream, StriVectin-SD, which was developed by Klein-Becker for Sephora. Designed to be a cream to eliminate stretch marks, it quickly was adapted by consumers to combat facial wrinkles and sagging. Within a very short period, it quickly became one of the top sellers in US department stores, online, and specialty stores in the prestige skincare industry.

In the LVMH 2004 Annual Report, LVMH too was celebrating Levy's operational successes, stating, "Sephora had an excellent year in 2004 and achieved all of its objectives. The brand recorded strong growth in sales and profitability, in both Europe and the United States, and generated positive cash flow, which will continue to finance its expansion." As of December 31, 2004, Sephora had achieved a global network of 521 stores, opened eight new stores in Europe, twelve more in the US, and finally had a breakthrough with Spain, signing a partnership agreement with El Corte Ingles department store chain. Most impressive, however, was how well Sephora was doing in the US. For the fourth consecutive year, Sephora recorded double-digit sales growth, "well above trends in the selective retailing industry."[21]

In the same annual report, LVMH attributed various reasons for the robust growth, namely the new strategy to position the company as being "synonymous with innovation and expertise in beauty products."[22] Then it highlighted examples that this strategy was working, noting "exclusive agreements of a number of trendsetting perfume and makeup brands and of skincare products that provide real added value. The development of innovative services was another contributing factor. Sephora strengthened its partnership with leading perfume and cosmetics brands and its original media and promotional policy, while continuing to develop several product lines under its own brand that combine creativity, quality, and attractive prices."[23]

Expanding Beyond Cosmetics to Skincare and Services

Infused with more money and buoyed by the runaway success of Sephora Collection and StriVectin-SD, Sephora launched its own skincare line in 2005, with affordably priced products ranging from the three to twenty-five dollars, with everything from cleansers to masks to serums and night creams. By comparison, some skincare lines can exceed upward of five hundred dollars per jar of moisturizer. (Le Mer's Crème de le Mer goes as high as five hundred and ten dollars a jar.) Giving their customers more affordable options proved to be both a profitable move and a long-term strategy as well. By having a lower-cost option in a luxury brand store, they could essentially groom a whole new generation of young buyers to become familiar with luxury brands featured along with the affordably priced Sephora Collection. Levy and his team were playing the long game.

In the same year, Sephora rolled out a range of in-store services—hairstyling, brow shaping/waxing, nails, and makeup tutorials and services. It also was expanding in Eastern Europe, purchasing Empik perfume chain in Poland and creating a partnership with Russian perfumery L'Etoile. They also entered into the Chinese market in a joint venture with Shanghai Jahwa United. By the end of 2005, Sephora had three stores in Shanghai. By the beginning of 2006, Sephora was the only selective retailing perfumery present on three continents and was growing in profitability across the board.

According to the LVMH 2006 Annual Report, thanks in large part to the revenue growth, expansion, profitability, "Sephora exceeded its goals on both sides of the Atlantic." In the same report it formally announced its first store opening in the Middle East as well. In just one year, Sephora had grown from a global network of 521 stores to 621 stores. While expanding it was also taking on massive renovations to its older stores. But, perhaps one of its most interesting plays was the unexpected partnership with US retailer JCPenney.

Sephora Partners with JCPenney

JCPenney doesn't exactly scream "luxury items" or even carry many of the upscale LVMH brands. When people think of JCPenney they are more likely to think *mark down* than *Marc Jacobs*. It's the store our moms bought towels, holiday-themed pajamas, ill-fitting cardigans, and sensible shoes for work. This isn't some overly pretentious and judgy writer's perspective. JCPenney Co. was well aware of their aging demographics and their dowdy image. In 2004, JCPenney hired a new Chairman and Chief Executive Myron E. "Mike" Ullman III, who was intent on changing the store's image and began offering more upscale brand names in order to attract a new generation into their stores (to actually shop, not walk through). As a part of this new image, they announced their partnership with Sephora in April 2006.

At the time, JCPenney operated over one thousand stores through the US (there are now approximately eleven hundred), no small market, so it would be advantageous for Sephora as well. With JCPenney, Sephora could expand their footprint and reach a larger demographic outside of urban areas and upscale malls. Under the agreement, each Sephora shop would be featured in a visible and prominent location at the center of the department store, and it would also include the same back-lit display cases and sample products that are featured in stand-alone Sephora stores. Additionally, each Sephora "store-within-a-store" would have salespeople who were trained as Sephora employees. It was a unique and otherwise unheard of approach at the time.[24]

Today, we take the "store-within-a-store" or "pop up" concept for granted. It's become hugely popular over the last decade. We absolutely expect to find Starbucks *everywhere*—at Target, at our grocery stores, and even Macy's. Truly, grocery stores were really the first adopters—opening stand-alone pharmacies within their stores. But it's extended far beyond implementing pharmacies and coffee shops into major retailers thanks in large part to Sephora's success in JCPenney. Samsung Experience stores opened in 2013 in Best Buys across the country. In 2018, Nordstrom announced that it was now partnering with the high-end, boho-chic clothing and furnishing retailer Anthropologie, who would now have a prominent section in their department stores across the country. Macy's also uses the "store-within-a-store" model to attract a different demographic of customers, and now hosts the athletic shoe store Finish Line and Sunglass Huts along with Starbucks in many of their stores.

According to Kevin Marschall, vice president of retail advisory and transaction services at the CBRE Group, a store-within-a-store can be a "win-win situation" for the both retailer and the tenant. For the host retailer, like JCPenney, a store-within-a-store offers the opportunity "to enhance their experience and attract customers who are eager to learn more about a particular product or brand."[25] And for the tenant, like Sephora, it offers them a "better location than a standalone store and with low risk, low overhead and minimal startup costs. It can be a relatively easy and cost-effective way to gain access to prime real estate almost overnight, promote new products and experiment with marketing strategies."[26] At the time, David Suliteanu, who was the then president and CEO of Sephora Americas, stated the reason Sephora partnered with JCPenney was because "JCPenney's focus on providing relevant merchandise to its broad customer base is consistent with our objectives. This includes America's youngest women, a market in which JCPenney is a significant and rapidly growing factor."[27]

By opening sixty Sephora stores in JCPenneys across the country, Sephora was quickly able to expand their demographic reach. And JCPenney could as well, since Sephora appealed to a younger demographic of shoppers who normally wouldn't shop at JCPenney. It was, according to Ken Morris, principal at Boston Retail Partners, "a great way to extend their customer base and drive more traffic to their stores."[28] Today Sephora is located in almost 650 of JCPenney's stores across the country. In addition to its physical presence, Sephora is the exclusive online beauty product seller on JC-Penney's website.

> " By opening sixty Sephora stores in JCPenneys across the country, Sephora was quickly able to expand their demographic reach. And JCPenney could as well, since Sephora appealed to a younger demographic of shoppers who normally wouldn't shop at JCPenney.

Where Sephora *Wasn't*

By the end of 2006, Sephora seemed to be everywhere—in malls, upscale shopping areas around the world, and even where we wouldn't expect it, JCPenney. All around the world, Sephora was growing. Even Spain, which was slow to start, was experiencing double-digit growth. In addition to its physical presence across the globe, Sephora was focusing on its online presence—including the creation of Sephora.fr website for the

French market. The US website sephora.com was also experiencing major growth.

Most noticeably missing from the Sephora expansion in Europe was still the UK. To this day it is absent from the UK. In a cheekily titled article for *Grazia*, "Sephora Sadly Won't Be Coming to the UK After All," beauty writer Katie Rosseinsky assuages distraught UK beauty buyers after finding out that the word on the street that Sephora was going to open a store London's Westfield was indeed just a rumor. She writes, "Sad, we won't have access to Sephora's face masks, lipsticks and foundations anytime soon as the whispers were not true."[29] Sephora, for their part, was tightlipped about why they weren't opening stores or a website for UK consumers and gave no comments to reporters inquiring about their absence. This fact, however, didn't deter UK Sephora fans. Several beauty bloggers advised fellow Sephora devotees how to get the goods, namely by purchasing them from the US website and paying the pricey cost of shipping.

However, in July 2018, Sephora announced it would no longer be shipping to the UK. In an article for *Cosmopolitan*, "Sephora is No Longer Shipping to the UK," writer Laura Capon bemoaned the bad news: "Today is the worst, the actual worst. All hope is gone, all happiness lost, because today is the day the UK customers can no longer order from the Sephora US website."[30] Instead UK and Netherlands customers were redirected to Sephora France, which according to Capon, "doesn't stock half the brands as their US counterpart." Capon ended her article with, "It's a dark day in the beauty world."[31] Hyperbole aside, all of this is to say that even where Sephora isn't there is a premium on the brand. Their reputation precedes them, and even those who don't get to shop either in stores or online have a strong desire to do so. This all is in large part due to a consistent strategy to woo customers and keep them coming back for more, or in the case of the UK, simply begging them to come to them.

The Pillars of Sephora's Early Success— Building Customer Loyalty

In the 2006 LVMH Annual Report, Sephora highlighted their "strategy of differentiation and building customer loyalty," and attributed it to several pillars: "an innovative and high-quality selection of exclusive brands that meet high expectations, such as StriVectin-SD (anti-wrinkle care) and Bare Escentuals (mineral makeup); forming dynamic partnerships with the inescapable large brands in the selective world of perfume and cosmetics; strengthening its positioning as a beauty expert, illustrated by the development of innovative services; and welcoming spaces, such as Sephora Studio, a dispenser of care and wellness."[32] The report also extolled how well Sephora had increased its visibility on the three continents "by advertising through numerous media (billboards, press, radio, television, Internet, mailings)" and that it even was advertising in movie theaters in France.[33]

With its retail store's visibility and brand recognition at an all-time high, the annual report also highlighted Sephora's own cosmetic brand and remarked how it "continues to successfully renew and develop the high-quality products that are sold at especially attractive prices."[34] All of these successes, in both their retail store and their own cosmetic line, were buttressed, the report indicated, "by steady investment in the training of advisors and store managers: there is an in-house school on each of the three continents where Sephora operates."[35] Sephora believed the key to maintain loyalty was guaranteeing customers had a positive experience while in Sephora.

Finally, the report mentioned its loyalty card as a "key component of a close relationship with its customers" and believed it played a key role in leading Sephora to expand it to virtually every country in Europe. It also announced in the same report that they planned on rolling out this same program in the US in 2007 and hoped to see similar results.

> Sephora highlighted their "strategy of differentiation and building customer loyalty," and attributed it to several pillars: "an innovative and high-quality selection of exclusive brands that meet high expectations, such as StriVectin-SD (anti-wrinkle care) and Bare Escentuals (mineral makeup); forming dynamic partnerships with the inescapable large brands in the selective world of perfume and cosmetics; strengthening its positioning as a beauty expert, illustrated by the development of innovative services; and welcoming spaces, such as Sephora Studio, a dispenser of care and wellness."

Sephora's US Beauty Insider Program

Over the past decade, the loyalty card has expanded and now boasts over ten million card holders in the US alone. It is considered to be "one of the most well-known rewards programs in both the retail and ecommerce loyalty communities," according to writer Alex McEachern, an ecommerce and retention marketing expert and founder of Spark Retention and Marketing, who wrote the loyalty case study on Sephora. McEachern attributes the success of the loyalty program to its effective use of tiers. "By breaking customers into distinct groups, you can use each tier to challenge the shopper to see if they can reach the next milestone. Tiers can be set based on number of orders, loyalty points earned, or dollars spent, and Sephora has chosen to use the dollars spent method within their loyalty program."[36]

As a Sephora loyalty card holder, the owner becomes what is called a "Beauty Insider." The Beauty Insider Program is Sephora's free rewards program in the United States and Canada and it lets customers earn points on all the merchandise purchases and redeemed those points for rewards. For every US (or Canadian dollar) spent on Sephora merchandise online at Sephora.com or Sephora.ca, in retail stores, or even inside JCPenney or on JCPenney.com (on Sephora merchandise only), card members earn according to their spending status. A Beauty Insider earns 1 point for every dollar, a Beauty Insider with VIB status (Very Important Beauty Insider, who spends more than 350 dollars a year) earns 1.25 points for every dollar, and the Rouge Status card holder (who spends more than one thousand dollars in a year) earns 1.5 points for every dollar spent. In addition to rewards, customers have their own "Beauty Insider Page" online, where they can review their year-to-date activity, current points balance, and redeem their points for rewards and benefits.[37]

Another way Sephora's rewards program gets it right according to McEachern's case study, is its "rewards match the brand and customer base." He writes, "Sephora has done an excellent job aligning their rewards with what the brand stands for. The Sephora brand has become synonymous with prestige, quality, and luxury—all of which are reflected in what they offer as customer rewards."[38] For example, VIB Rouge members, he says, are given the chance to earn rewards like exclusive products and events, access to the Sephora Beauty Studio, and early access to products and sales. McEachern writes, "Sephora's Beauty Insider Program is seen as a high-end or luxurious program, and they have created a redemption process that reflects that. Instead of using points for a discount, Beauty Insider members can use their points to claim more beauty products at the Rewards Bazaar." McEachern argues this is "on brand" with Sephora because discounts and coupons are not typically associated with "premium or luxury brands."[39]

The third reason why Sephora's loyalty brand is so successful, the case study concludes, is because of their personalized product recommendations. "Sephora knows that their shoppers are highly motivated by experiences, which is clear through how they set up their tiers and rewards," McEachern asserts. "The desire for experiences is also why they have created personalized product recommendations for Beauty Insider members."[40]

Furthermore, the product recommendations are tailored to each customer based on their shopping history. While this a great feature for consistent or regular shoppers, whose data is aggregated and collected over time, for new shoppers, this isn't always easy. That is why Sephora offers a "Beauty Profile" for their online shoppers. A customer simply answers some questions about their eyes, complexion, and skin type, and an algorithm is able to offer suggestions on personalized products based on the information provided.

> **Sephora has done an excellent job aligning their rewards with what the brand stands for. The Sephora brand has become synonymous with prestige, quality, and luxury—all of which are reflected in what they offer as customer rewards."**

Though the case study cited a few areas where Sephora could improve their loyalty rewards program, most notably by making the signup more prominent on their home page, the author of it concluded it by stating, "Sephora's Beauty Insider Program is without a doubt one of the best examples of a loyalty program in existence. It's successful both in store and online."[41]

Nearing the ten-year mark with LVMH in 2007, Sephora had continued to dominate the market share. With a global reach, a brand that had become the envy of retailers, and a loyal customer base, Sephora had grown from a small boutique perfumery to a beauty powerhouse that captured the hearts of millions of shoppers across the world. But perhaps their greatest asset was their commitment to innovation and adapting to not just the retail environment but the cosmetics and beauty industry to the digital age.

"I believe that if you're going to be a successful retailer—or business in general—digital must be enmeshed at the highest level."

—JULIE BORNSTEIN,
former chief marketing officer & chief digital officer, Sephora

CHAPTER THREE

INNOVATION IN SELLING COSMETICS, SKINCARE, HAIRCARE

While LVMH was celebrating ten years with Sephora and reporting record gains in 2007, the global financial crisis was just beginning. Soon after Lehman Brothers' announcement of their own collapse on September 15, 2008, the US stock market crashed and global markets soon followed, leading the world into the Great Recession for the next several years. Areas first affected were the housing markets and banking, but soon all major industries were impacted. The unemployment rate skyrocketed, and so too did evictions, foreclosures, and household debt. Declines in consumer wealth were estimated in the trillions in the US alone.[1] Credit availability was at an all-time low and overall international trade declined as well. However, one area that seemed to be unscathed by the economic downturn was the beauty industry.

In his 2008 LVMH Annual Report, Bernard Arnault said, "The 2008 results demonstrate the exceptional reactivity of our organization in this period of economic crisis. The group has always emerged stronger from previous economic downturns thanks to the dynamic innovation of its brands, the quality of its products and the effectiveness of its teams. LVMH approaches the challenges and the opportunities of 2009 with confidence and determination and has set the objective of increasing its leadership position in the worldwide luxury goods sector." Included in his highlights, he reported record increase revenue and profits, continued growth across all major brands, "excellent performance" of the Perfumes and Cosmetics groups and Sephora. While the world markets were crashing, LVMH Selective Retailing group (which included Sephora) registered organic revenue growth of 9 percent. And despite the economic crisis, Sephora still had plans to grow and expand in key market areas. It also boasted growth in online sales in France, the US, and China. Finally, the report attributed Sephora's success to its "continued differentiation strategy with a more innovative and exclusive product offering, complemented by a large range of in-store services and treatments."[2]

End of the Levy Era and Leadership Transitions

But the company was also going through transition internally. Levy stepped down as CEO of Sephora in March of 2011, and passed away shortly after from a long illness on January 1, 2012.[3] On March 31, 2011 Christopher de Lapuente, who led P&G's global hair care division and served in various capacities there for twenty-eight years, became the global president and

CEO for Sephora. Bernard Arnault, LVMH founder, chairman and CEO, was hopeful about the new leader and was counting on his international experience to help with their expansion goals, stating, "Joining LVMH as a member of the executive committee and head of Sephora, Christopher de Lapuente will bring to the group a wealth of international experience; his know-how will be a precious asset for the global growth of Sephora and add to the continued success of LVMH."[4]

Kendo Brands & Global Celebrity Partnership with Rihanna

Soon after, Lapuente began to make organizational shifts. In 2014, he asked David Suliteanu, who had successfully led Sephora Americas since 2001 through a period of rapid expansion, to become the CEO of Kendo Brands, which is the LVMH "Beauty Brand Incubator." Kendo is a play on the words for "can do" and is the creativity hub for the next generation of beauty product development for global Sephora channels and selective retailers outside of Sephora. Suliteanu was asked to lead the San Francisco-based Kendo to help develop, collaborate, and acquire new brands for LVMH, that at the time included Bite, Kat Von D, and Marc Jacobs Beauty. Shortly after taking charge at Kendo, Suliteanu partnered with pop star, model, entrepreneur, and beauty vlogger Rihanna to launch a unique inclusive cosmetic line, Fenty Beauty, designed to match every single skin tone. It debuted to wide acclaim and sensational sales in 2017 (over one hundred million dollars in sales in the first few weeks).[5]

Everything Rihanna touches turned to gold, or should we say: *Platinum.* She is the youngest solo artist to achieve fourteen number one singles. She has sold more than 250 million records worldwide, and has won nine Grammys, twelve Billboard Music Awards, and thirteen American Music Awards. *Forbes* has ranked her among the top ten highest-paid celebrities and she was named by *Time* in both 2012 and 2018 as one of the 100 Most Influential People in the world, thanks in large part to her impressive social media following, even by celebrity standards. She has over 6.5 million followers on YouTube alone. Today, her official Instagram account, Fenty Beauty by Rihanna, has over 8.5 million followers, which has the second largest following of LVMH cosmetic brands (Benefit has 9.7 million followers). At the time of the signing, Suliteanu had high hopes for the brand, "Fenty Beauty by Rihanna is a beauty rocket ship that will appeal to a huge and diverse global audience. We are aiming for the stars."[6]

> Suliteanu partnered with pop star, model, entrepreneur, and beauty vlogger Rihanna to launch a unique inclusive cosmetic line, Fenty Beauty, designed to match every single skin tone. It debuted to wide acclaim and sensational sales in 2017 (over one hundred million dollars in sales in the first few weeks).

Suliteanu's expectations were on target. Within one year of Fenty Beauty's launch in 2017, Fenty Beauty reportedly made 570 million dollars in sales in its first fifteen months—nearly a tenth of LVMH's entire perfume and cosmetic line, which includes established brands like Guerlain, Acqua Di Parma, Parfums Christian Dior, Givenchy Parfums, Perfumes Loewe, Benefit Cosmetics, Makeup For Ever, Kenzo Parfums, Fresh, Kat Von Beauty, Maison Francis Kurkdjian, Marc Jacobs Beauty, and Cha Ling. The entire Fenty Beauty operation is said to be worth three billion dollars.[7] According to *Forbes*, Rihanna is now the "World's Richest Female Musician" and is said to have amassed over six hundred million dollars. For those keeping count, that's more than Queen B's fortune. (Beyoncé's net worth tally is four hundred million dollars sans her husband Jay-Z's billion-dollar fortune according to *Forbes*.)[8]

The decision to partner with, and launch, Rihanna's Fenty Beauty is a testament to the power of celebrities not just with massive followings—but ones with an iconic and inclusive brand. Rihanna reaches out to all generations, all races, and all backgrounds. By releasing forty shades of foundation, she and her brand, according to Stephanie Wissink, a research analyst for Jeffries, "challenged the standard convention that you only needed a very defined set of shades to satisfy a market. Not only did Fenty Beauty achieve meaningful sales, but it potentially changed the industry permanently."[9] That's exactly what Rihanna hoped to do when she launched her beauty line in the first place, saying on LVMH.com, "Fenty Beauty was created for everyone: for women of all shades, personalities, attitudes, cultures, and races. I wanted everyone to feel included. That's the real reason I made this line."

In 2018, LVMH extended an offer to Rihanna to reach beyond her cosmetics brand and to join their fashion house and become the first black woman to run a major luxury fashion house and the first new LVMH house in more than thirty years. In an interview with the *New York Times Style Magazine*, Rihanna said, "They extended the offer to me and it was a no-brainer because LVMH is a machine. Bernard Arnault was so enthusiastic; he trusted me and my vision."[10] Keeping with her inclusive ideal, the new luxury brand has sizes that go up to a US 14. Wissink believes that Rihanna is poised to shake up the fashion world, just like she did the beauty world. "What Fenty Beauty did to beauty, Fenty lifestyle is going to do to fashion. It's going to raise the bar for what it looks like to build a brand that's inclusive, game changing, global and iconic."

Inclusive, game changing, global, and iconic are certainly words the Sephora brand wants to be associated with. It was hoping to capitalize on being a leader in these areas, and it was hoping do so with its new leaders.

> **The decision to partner with and launch Rihanna's Fenty Beauty is a testament to the power of celebrities not just with massive followings—but ones with an iconic and inclusive brand. Rihanna reaches out to all generations, all races, and all backgrounds. By releasing forty shades of foundation, she and her brand, according to Stephanie Wissink, a research analyst for Jeffries, "challenged the standard convention that you only needed a very defined set of shades to satisfy a market."**

Calvin McDonald
Heads Up Sephora Americas

Lapuente then hired Calvin McDonald to take over for Suliteanu as CEO of Sephora Americas' role. In the press release announcing his new role, McDonald was lauded by his new employer, "In addition to his focus on exceptional consumer experiences, he is known for his collaborative leadership skills, strong vendor relationships, and ability to drive revenue while managing businesses efficiently and effectively."[11] Prior to joining Sephora Americas, McDonald served as the president and CEO of Sears Canada in 2011, (the separately listed Canadian business of Sears). According to a Sephora press release, he was tasked with "turning around the business [Sears Canada], which had lost more than $1 billion in revenues (bringing it to $4.5 billion) and had seen significant gross margin decline." During this time, he successfully led employees across both its retail and direct businesses, and developed a "transformation growth plan focused on product, innovation and improving culture."[12] LVMH was counting on McDonald's abilities in business growth, leadership, and innovation. In a statement, Lapuente said, "Calvin McDonald has established himself as a visionary and highly talented industry leader at two of Canada's largest and most important retailers. We are delighted to welcome him to Sephora Americas. He will focus on building on the extraordinary growth of the business in new and existing markets and continue Sephora's exceptional track record of industry leadership driven by David Suliteanu."[13]

McDonald added, "It is thrilling to be joining Sephora Americas, which is known across the retail industry for not only having revolutionized the beauty business but also for delivering a consistent stream of innovation in terms of merchandise, experience and digital capabilities that excite and inspire customers. I am looking forward to working with the exceptional Sephora team to build on what they have accomplished under David's leadership. Sephora Americas is an amazing success story, and I am proud and privileged to work with our cast members, brand partners and customers and colleagues worldwide as we work to take Sephora Americas to the next level of innovation and growth."[14]

That "next level" of innovation and growth went hand-in-hand with the rapidly changing digital world.

Sephora's Digital Transformation

Sephora was an early e-commerce adopter when it launched its first website in 1998. But, their transformation and adaption to the mobile revolution is due in large part to the leadership of Julie Bornstein, who was hired by Suliteanu to be Sephora's CMO & chief digital officer in 2007. According to a 2014 Harvard Business article "How Sephora Reorganized to Become a More Digital Brand," Daniel McGinn interviewed Bornstein, and asked her how she updated Sephora and brought it into the digital age.

"It's hard to imagine now," Bornstein recalls, "but I joined Sephora when mobile shopping was something of the future. E-commerce players were still figuring things out, and brick-and-mortar stores weren't really experimenting with technology. Yet based on my own experiences, I believed we could use technology to make shopping more efficient." She went on to explain that the original Sephora.com was largely outsourced and she didn't even have an internal development team when she joined. Bornstein explained that one of the first things she did when she came on board was to bring web development in-house, adding, "I'd recommend [bringing web development in-house] to any who's serious about building a digital brand.[15] The reason for doing so was because she recognized the need for a "stronger, more flexible foundation in order to drive digital into the future."[16]

A crucial part of building an in-house web department was building the talent that could execute it. "We scouted the right talent, and put in the blood, sweat and tears," Bornstein explained. "We later re-launched the website, taking it far beyond product specs and shopping carts. We built something that would give our clients access to better images, better information about products, and ways to communicate with each other. We're constantly evolving mobile and web experiences to stay current and adjust based on our own analytics. Having an in-house team is critical."[17]

Besides having an in-house team that could be agile, flexible, and work immediately to meet the needs of customers, Bornstein attributed their holistic approach to digital as the true key to their success. "Not even a decade ago, companies like Nordstrom ran Nordstrom.com as an entirely separate business. The impact that had on the operations and culture was significant. At the time, it served an important role, and that was to create a start-up within an established company. The companies that did this have much bigger online businesses today. But ultimately, that structure isn't customer centric. Digital being silo'd today is the result of legacy brands tacking on digital. But I believe that if you're going to be a successful retailer—or business in general—digital must be enmeshed at the highest level." Having digital "enmeshed at the highest level" however wasn't easy, she adds. "It required significant shifts in our own thinking, in structure, and in hiring the right talent. And because of that, we're far better set-up for success."[18]

Change isn't always easy, and there is always resistance. For a company that had been so focused for years on the in-store experience, getting everyone at Sephora onboard to think "digitally" required a new way to approach the customer. In her mind, it was simple and in some ways very similar to the way Sephora's founder Mandonnaud had approached retail when he first started: Put the customer at the center of the experience. "We also try to think like customers—how would I want to shop, what would make my experience better, how do my kids' interactions with technology predict the future? And then we brainstorm. Marketing and internal IT expertise are both at the table. Each group can imagine things are possible that the other might not have dreamed of," Bornstein explains. "Unfortunately at many big organizations, some of the best ideas never come to fruition because the right IT expertise isn't there. We're lucky to have an amazing CTO with a deep knowledge of e-commerce and strong desire to partner with the business, and a strong team behind him."[19]

> " For a company that had been so focused for years on the in-store experience, getting everyone at Sephora onboard to think "digitally" required a new way to approach the customer.

She also is proud of the fact that when others in the beauty retail industry were purporting that mobile was best served as "a content engine" and "mobile shopping would take years to take off," Sephora "dove-in head first." She adds, "We were one of the first to develop a mobile site, and mobile sales have grown +100% each year in the past three years. You have to back-up the hunches with the right talent and right investments. For us, it's paid off."[20]

> **"** She also is proud of the fact that when others in the beauty retail industry were purporting that mobile was best served as "a content engine" and "mobile shopping would take years to take off," Sephora "dove-in head first."

When asked how she specifically was able to pull it off, she explained, "We re-established structure between traditional marketing and digital marketing teams. That may seem easy, but anyone who's run a large organization knows it's no small feat. It required months of planning and puzzle-solving." This too, she admitted, was not easy and a "work in progress" at the time of the interview. "By merging teams, we make the most of our investments across all channels and do things more efficiently, more powerfully. We also move faster—which, in this day and age, is what makes all the difference. I firmly believe that this will be the way of the future. Marketing and digital must be hand-in-hand."[21]

Bornstein argues in the article that most companies should have a tightly integrated chief digital officer and chief marketing officer, if not one-in-the-same. "An analytics and creative organization support both the e-commerce and store marketing efforts. . . . It won't just help operationally; it will impact the bottom line."[22]

Another challenge of adopting to the digital age was simply keeping up since the pace of the digital age was lightning fast. "There will always be something else to solve, something else to build," Bornstein says. "There will always be a new Pinterest, a new Instagram, a new desire from your customers to connect. And as the next generation of shoppers grows up, they'll have different needs as well. We're constantly evaluating new technologies and platforms. Sephora is headquartered in San Francisco, where we eat, breathe, and live digital. We can test things early, and help influence the design. The minute we stop looking for the next consumer touchpoint is the minute we become like those who said 'mobile shopping will never exist.'"[23]

Being on the lookout for the next consumer touchpoint required a new way to approach their business structure, namely by becoming what they termed an "Omni Experience and Innovation" leader in the industry.

Omnichannel Leader

Over the next several years, Sephora double-downed on innovation and expansion and by 2016, especially in the US, it represented 45 percent of all LVMH's business—for all their groups. It had also continued to grow online and was now available in Singapore, Scandinavia, Switzerland, Mexico, and the Middle East (United Arab Emirates).[24] Their physical footprint increased as well, opening stores in Germany for the first time in 2017 and then in India in 2018, with its sights set on New Zealand. In their 2017 Annual Report, LVMH once again reported double-digit revenue growth and gained market share worldwide for its Sephora group, stating: "Its particularly remarkable performance in the United States propelled the brand to the highest echelon of the selective beauty market." It also inaugurated several iconic locations, including La Canopée in Paris and the newly opened World Trade Center in New York City.[25] They attributed this success this time to "digital engagement and services" noting that "The brand's strategy was more omni-channel [sic] than ever, with efforts focused on developing mobile applications, offering in-store digital features and reducing delivery time."[26] This is the first time that the reports use the term *omnichannel* in regard to Sephora's strategy.

Omnichannel is a word to describe the cross-channel content and physical strategy that most companies or organizations employ to provide better experiences for their customers. It's considered to be an interactive communication and business strategy that uses several channels as a means to support one another and be more cooperative rather than competitive. In other words, Sephora's online channel doesn't compete with Sephora in-store retail experience rather it helps *support* the consumer experience by enhancing their ability to shop where and when it is most convenient for them. Channels can include but are not limited to physical locations (stand-alone stores and store-within-a-store), online, mobile apps, and even social media.

Sephora had long been in on the omnichannel game. As mentioned earlier, it was one of the first retailers to launch a retail website in 1998, and later, as retail was taking a hit after the Great Recession and most brick and mortar shops were closing up and moving strictly into the online retail space,

Sephora continued to expand in the physical retail space. But it took the omnichannel game one step further in 2015, when it launched its Sephora Innovation Lab in the Dogpatch neighborhood of San Francisco. The new physical office space was also a place that offered programs that would, according to the press release announcing itself to the world, "foster the culture of innovation and development along with the grooming of Sephora's next generation of leaders."[27]

On the Search for Newest and Best Technologies

Excited about the new venture, President and CEO Calvin McDonald stated, "Innovation has always been in our DNA. We disrupted beauty by being the first to offer clients access to premium beauty out from behind the department store make-up counters, and we want to keep that spirit and bold tenacity alive. The new Lab will tap the collective creativity of our fourteen thousand employees nationwide, grow the next generation of leaders, and elevate Sephora's digital future."[28]

According to McDonald, the Innovation Lab would be a place where the team "can ideate, test, dream, experiment and learn. As new ideas surface, the Lab team will be responsible for sourcing, developing, evaluating, testing and eventually launching new offerings and technologies for shopping in the store and on-the-go."[29] In the announcement, he stated that it had teamed up with Google, Apple, and others in the past, and further planned to "evaluate additional strategic alliances in the future, through the Lab program."[30]

In addition to new technologies and alliances, Sephora also announced that it already had created a think tank program in the Innovation Lab that would "groom the next generation of leaders, who will be developing the 'next big idea' in retail."[31] This think tank team meets monthly and works to solve for "the way we shop five years from now," according to McDonald.[32]

In addition to the think tank, the Lab would also oversee what it called "Idea Central," an employee-driven idea program that gathered ideas from all employees nationwide regardless of their function within the company.[33]

"We're completely focused on making shopping more efficient, intelligent and fun for our clients," said Bornstein about the announcement of the Innovation Lab. "We spend a lot of time walking in the shoes of our clients as inspiration for dreaming up new technologies and partnering with technology companies in the Bay Area to develop innovative solutions for new ways to shop."

In the announcement of the Innovation Lab, it also unveiled four specific digital experiences created by the Lab already. The first was the use of beacons, or a personalized alert system for clients who opted in. Shoppers could receive birthday alerts, loyalty program updates, and be notified of trainings and ongoing services on their phones while in the store. Another was a "Pocket Contour" experience. Getting onboard the Kardashian-fueled contour craze, Sephora partnered up with Map My Beauty, which according to the press release was "the first-of-its-kind cross-platform personal virtual make-up artist application."[34] By analyzing a photo on mobile, the app can help beauty consumers identify their face-shape, and give them a personalized step-by-step guidance on how to apply make-up with a contoured look they wanted to achieve.

They also announced that they would soon be offering an augmented reality feature via the Sephora-to-Go mobile app for iPhone. With the app clients would be able to engage with custom content by hovering over various brand founder faces, like Laura Mercier, Josie Maran, Kat Von D, and others featured in the Sephora windows and display cases. By scanning each image with their phones, customers could experience interviews with brand founders, product videos, animated GIFs, various YouTube playlists, and product pages on Sephora.com, all without leaving the app. And finally, it also announced Sephora Flash, which was designed for frequent shoppers. Those who signed up for Sephora Flash could enjoy free two-day shipping on all products and was free for Rouge Beauty Insider Members, much like the hugely popular Amazon Prime that offers free shipping to their Prime members as well.

"The Innovation Lab and dedicated management team gives us an incredible opportunity to drive the future of innovation," added Bridget Dolan, the then vice president of the Sephora Innovation Lab who was tasked with leading the Lab and team. "Given our location in the heart of the digital and tech scene, we have strong visibility into the players and trends, both on and offline, that could be molded into Sephora-centric experiences. We have a relentless hunger for developing technologies and networking with emerging technology companies that might seem unexpected now, but could define the future of retail."[35]

Rolling Out the New Technologies

Even before the Innovation Lab was officially called "the Innovation Lab" Sephora had been spending a considerable amount of time and resources dedicated to creating digital and tech-enabled experiences. One of the first was its Sephora-to-Go mobile app. "We recognized that mobile was the key to unifying our gifting program across all retail channels and supporting the omnichannel experience our customers were already seeking," said Dolan.[36] It had already become part of Apple's Passbook in 2012, but with the launch of the Sephora-to-Go app, they could leverage a cloud-based platform operated by CashStar, a mobile gifting app, to offer mobile digital gifting.

Instead of plastic gift cards, which up until then could not be redeemed online and were the bane of many a Sephora devotee's existence, Sephora could now offer digital gift cards. Dolan acknowledged that mobile shopping was an "important way in which customers were researching products, creating wish lists, and making purchases."[37] With this new technology offering, shoppers could send, redeem, and store digital and plastic gift cards in either the Sephora-to-Go mobile app or their preferred mobile wallet app, like Apple's Wallet. In addition to being able to send digital gifts from any tablet, smartphone, or computer, customers could also personalize their digital gift cards with their own preferred photos or videos. They could also upgrade their gifts and add Beauty Services eGift Cards, which awards the recipient with an in-store 45-minute makeover.[38]

> " Instead of plastic gift cards, which up until then could not be redeemed online and were the bane of many a Sephora devotee's existence, Sephora could now offer digital gift cards. Dolan acknowledged that mobile shopping was an "important way in which customers were researching products, creating wish lists, and making purchases."

Since implementing the mobile app, according to a study done by their vendor CashStar, Sephora digital gift cards "gained a higher initial value, faster redemption velocity and a higher basket value at redemption. But the most significant result was a Sephora digital gift card revenue growth that was eight times faster than the growth rate the prior year. Digital gift transactions also went up by 90 percent just one year after the program was launched."[39] Dolan considered this a huge success, further adding, "51 percent of our digital gift cards are redeemed within just one month, compared to 33 percent of our plastic gift cards. . . . We expect digital gifting to become a key differentiator for retailers working to drive omnichannel growth, and we look forward to staying at the forefront of this movement."[40] Sephora-to-Go is simply now called the Sephora app, where customers can shop, play with makeup virtually, view exclusives, check out the Rewards Bazaar, and even activate the "store mode."

Taking the App and Omnichannel Experience a Step Further

Today most companies we interact with have omnichannels and apps. Again, we take for granted that we can do everything from our banking to our grocery shopping either in person, online, and through apps. We can even complain about or rave about and communicate with companies via social media. But Sephora truly was on the vanguard of this approach, leading the way not just for the beauty and cosmetics industry, but retail as a whole.

In an October 2017 Glossy article "Sephora Head of Omnichannel Retail Mary Beth Laughton: 'We need to over-deliver,'"

Priya Rao interviewed the newly named head of Sephora's new division Omnichannel Retail. In the interview, Laughton explained her new position and said her goal was to fully wed Sephora in-store and e-commerce properties in order to offer customers a "full-fledged" omnichannel experience.

The "full-fledged" experience she was talking about specifically was launched in January 2018 and debuted as the Sephora Store Companion app which served what its name promised: an in-store shopping companion as soon as the customer enters the store. "It puts past purchase information and personalized product recommendations at their fingertips," says Rao.[41] Rao also explains how Sephora also partnered with Google to bring the Google Assistant and Sephora's popular YouTube content together on the Google Home Hub voice assistant device. "I have been in this role for a little over a year, and pulling our stores and digital groups together with our consumer at the center has been our biggest accomplishment," Laughton contends. "The whole philosophy starts with doing what is right for the consumer and making easy, personalized experiences for her across our channels."[42]

> ❝ The whole philosophy starts with doing what is right for the consumer and making easy, personalized experiences for her across our channels."

Describing how Sephora's integration of the in-store experience and digital experience helped both sides of the business, Laughton says: "In today's retail environment, 'omnitude,' or approaching everything from the omnichannel perspective, is really critical because our consumer has high expectations. We cannot just deliver, but we need to over-deliver and make it really great for her. We want to serve the client the best way we can, regardless of where she is shopping with us."[43]

She added that Sephora recognized that "mobile is now at the center of everyone's life" and was the main driver of consumer behavior. Using the data they have captured from their various touchpoints, Sephora knows not just where their customers shop, but what they buy and how they go about it. "Our consumer starts with researching at home or on the bus on her way to work on our app," she explains. "Then, oftentimes, clients do make their first purchase in brick-and-mortar stores. We see a mixture, though: Some shoppers only shop with us in the physical setting, while others see the store as an introduction—where she gets familiar with our brand—and then do all of their shopping online."[44]

> " She added that Sephora recognized that "mobile is now at the center of everyone's life" and was the main driver of consumer behavior. Using the data they have captured from their various touchpoints, Sephora knows not just where their customers shop, but what they buy and how they go about it.

In a further effort to link both the physical and online experiences for the customer, Sephora launched "Happening at

Sephora." While it is a digital hub, it is linked to the retail environment in that, Laughton says, "it showcases everything happening in our physical stores, like events, classes, services and brand launches. . . . And then, of course, when she is in the store, there are a lot of digital tools that draw back to that experience."

Adding Digital Tools to the Physical

One thing Sephora has managed to do well as an omnichannel leader is bring the digital to physical. In addition to their Sephora app and Happening at Sephora digital hub and other simulation feature, Sephora also launched a Sephora Virtual Artist app, an augmented reality application available in select stores. Customers could "snap and try," meaning they can take a photo of virtually anyone's look by uploading an image of it and layer it over their own face. Customers can also "try on" a bunch of Sephora Collection products.

However exciting for the company, this new technology did invite a whole new level of unforeseen complications. In 2018, an Illinois woman sued Sephora and Modiface, Inc. (the software company that creates an augmented reality platform that enables beauty look try-on simulations) for what she alleges is a "violation of her privacy" and claims the Virtual Artist "take more than pictures." According to the *Cook Country Record*, Auste Salkauskaite filed a complaint individually and on behalf of similarly "situated individuals" in the Cook County Circuit Court, citing the Illinois Biometric Information Privacy Act.[45]

The plaintiff alleged that when she entered the Virtual Artist Kiosk, she was "required" to give personal information and that information was "disseminated in an attempt to sell her Sephora products."[46]

According to the records, Salkauskaite holds Sephora USA Inc. and Modiface Inc. responsible for failing to inform consumers in writing that their "biometrics were being collected and the terms under which their biometrics would be captured, collected, stored and used."[47] According to the record, the plaintiff requested a trial by jury, and seeks "injunctive and equitable relief, statutory damages; monetary damages, equitable relief, and punitive damages; and pre- and post-judgment interest."[48] As of this writing, the case is still ongoing and raises the questions: Are consumers aware of how their data is being collected? And do they understand that when they use such devices—or at any time interact with a company through any one of their channels—understand that is primarily for the purpose of data collection and further marketing?

> **The Biometric Information Privacy Act (BIPA) that was passed in Illinois in 2008 is the only law that allows private individuals to file a lawsuit for damages stemming from the violation. The BIPA requires that all companies doing business in Illinois comply to several requirements, among them are obtaining consent from individuals if the company intends to collect or disclose the identifiers, destroy biometric identifiers in timely manner, and securely store them.[49]**

Sephora made no comment to the *Cook County Record*. But it appears as though they are continuing to flight the claim, as the case was moved from the Cook County Circuit Court to the US District Court for the Northern District.

Despite dealing with the lawsuit, Sephora seems undeterred from bringing data and the digital experience into the physical environment. Another way they have brought the "digital to the physical" is by fully integrating otherwise physical experiences into the digital world. All Beauty Advisors (Sephora employees) are fully trained and all have mobile phones that allow them to interact with their customers. If a client is having a makeover done in-store, a Beauty Advisor can enter all the products used and send an email to the customer after the service, so if the customer wanted to they could reach out to the Beauty Advisor when she gets home or even buy more products. "It is about creating that personalized touch across all our channels," Laughton adds.[50]

Personalization and Creating a Customized Shopping Experience

Sephora isn't the only one who acknowledges personalization is an increasingly important trend in beauty. It's pretty much a trend *everywhere* and has been for the past two decades, and there are no signs that will change. Consumers have come to expect custom and personal experiences. We expect Netflix to queue up the next movie *they* think we will like best on our previous bingefest. We expect our phones to know we are headed to Starbucks every morning on our way into the office (and to let us know how many minutes it will take us to get there with traffic). We even expect our refrigerators to tell us we're short on almond milk and White Claw. There is no going back to the guesswork. We expect not just our friends and families to know us, but companies *and things* to know us as well.

Laughton believes, "The future is a very personal, in-person interaction that turns into a just-as-personal digital interaction, and vice versa."

 The future is a very personal, in-person interaction that turns into a just-as-personal digital interaction, and vice versa."

Sephora has responded to this need in a few different ways. First, like most companies, they use the data available from their CRM (Client Relationship Management) tool that tracks every touchpoint a customer has with Sephora. They gather everything—from where the customer came to the site (through an ad on Instagram, an influencer, a Google search, an article, an ad, an email campaign) to what pages they peruse, how much time they spend there, to what products they research, and even to what products they eventually put in their cart. Sephora is also able to capture data outside the scope of normal CRMs. They have other digital tools at their disposal as well. One in particular is their Color IQ device. Color IQ is a hand-held device only available in stores. Beauty Advisors are able to hold the device up to a customer's face and perfectly match his or her skin tone. Once the data is captured and added to the customer's Beauty Profile, Sephora can send emails, mobile push messages, or even offer complimentary products, with the best products that match his or her skin tone.[51]

Reaching Customers through Distributive Commerce

Another way they attempted to personalize and reach their customers is through what Laughton calls, "distributive commerce" or "this idea that customers want to increasingly engage with brands and retailers in the same way they engage with their friends."[52] That means "chat, text, social and voice assistance are where customers are spending their time, especially this younger generation."[53] Laughton recognizes that it is important for Sephora to be a leader in these channels. One way they have executed this is by being virtually omnipresent on social media, mainly through the use of influencers, beauty vloggers on YouTube, and bloggers who promote their products and store for them. But one of its key differentiators is that Sephora has also built its own community on its website, where shoppers can build their own profile, join groups and follow various topics and connect with fellow members, join conversations, ask questions, talk directly with brands, and keep up with breaking beauty and health news. It also has a complete photo gallery where community members can browse, post, and get inspiration based on the looks created by other members. Members also have access to exclusive events and "community meetups IRL" (in real life).

According to their Beauty Insider Community webpage, the community is, in their own words, "Real people. Real time. Real talk. Find beauty inspiration, ask questions and get recommendations from members like you. You ready?" There are over forty-two groups, ranging from "Skincare Aware" to "Everything Eyes" to "Best Hair Ever" to "Lip Lovers." There is also the popular "Trending Now" group that features the latest beauty updates and releases. Other groups are for those dealing with particular skincare issues, "Acne-Prone Skin," "Combination

Skins," "Oily Skins," "Dry Skins," and "Age Defiers." There are groups divided by lifestyle as well, "Makeup Minimalists" who like to keep their routine simple and "Savvy Shoppers" who are looking for deals, and even one for "Moms Only."

There are also inclusive groups like "Deeper Shades" for the "melanin blessed. Beauty Obsessed" as well as the "Trans is Beautiful" for the "Femme, mask, non-binary. Beauty your way." And there is even a "Men Who Makeup" group, which promotes itself as "Your favorite tool kit might be the one with a kabuki brush."

Their Customer Service group offers real-time live support between 6 a.m. and 10 p.m. PST Monday–Friday, 8am-9pm Saturday-Sunday. However, this seems more like a curse than a blessing for Sephora. On a quick glance of topics on their page, unhappy shoppers take their complaints to the public forum without a hint of reservation. One topic "$100 Rouge Award is Trash" is where several Sephora shoppers took their frustration with redeeming awards to the page. (Apparently, it's *quite* the issue.) "Frustration on 10. This is the 4th Tuesday I've used my lunch break to stalk the Reward Bazaar to cash in my points for the $100 Rouge Rewards and have failed. . . ." The poster whose handle is "Domos" wrote a lengthy post about her various attempts and failures to redeem her points. Others joined in sharing similar complaints and empathizing with Domos. And much like on other social media sites, group members can reply, view, and like.

For their part, Sephora customer service responds to and attempts to resolve these issues. It's gotta sting to see the proverbial dirty laundry hanging out for the neighbors to see, but the advantage of such a forum like this is Sephora hears about and can respond to customer issues in real time. Another advantage is, since only Beauty Insider Community members can follow the groups, it's not as public a forum as say Facebook or

Instagram—though shoppers certainly feel free to voice their opinions on those channels as well. Most of the groups, however, are positive, friendly, and helpful. Community members advise others on their purchases and what works for them, often influencing others to purchase their favorite products. Which of course, is the point.

" There are also inclusive groups like "Deeper Shades" for the "melanin blessed. Beauty Obsessed" as well as the "Trans is Beautiful" for the "Femme, mask, non-binary. Beauty your way." And there is even a "Men Who Makeup" group, which promotes itself as "Your favorite tool kit might be the one with a kabuki brush."

Using Influencers, Podcasts, and YouTube to Spread the Brand Message

If you happen to be one of those unicorns who has never been on social media or heard of influencers, they aren't employees at Sephora. In some cases they aren't even paid by Sephora (though there are professional paid/sponsored influencers as well). The majority of influencers, however, are what Sephora calls "microinfluencers" or regular people who try out products and share and post about their experiences on social media channels (Facebook, Twitter, Instagram, and Pinterest), and hashtag and/or mention their products and the #sephora name. Those who are paid influencers go through an extensive application process and are known officially as #SephoraSquad.

In February of 2019, a new round of paid influencers who were among fifteen thousand applicants were added to the diverse "squad." According to Elizabeth Segran, who covered Sephora's announcement for *Fast Company,* "In the past, Sephora has worked with influencers for smaller projects–like advertising campaigns, brand launches, and events. But #SephoraSquad will be a longer-term collaboration, one that allows the influencers to have much more autonomy in the content they create."

Deborah Yeh, Sephora's current CMO, says "that they will be tasked with talking about particular products or advertising campaigns. All of this will allow Sephora to embed itself in these smaller communities and be part of the conversations already happening online."[54] Yeh adds, "We want to hear from people in far-flung places. The more inclusive we are, the more we can represent the excitement and diversity that we see in beauty."[55]

In addition to paid influencers from a wide variety of backgrounds, lifestyles, and locations, as well as microinfluencers, Sephora has also taken on a multimedia approach as well, even getting in on the ever-popular podcast circuit. In 2018, they promoted their Sephora Collection's newest lipstick launch by partnering with Girlboss Media, to create an inspiring podcast called *#LIPSTORIES,* that highlighted stories of inspiring women leaders (*Girlbosses*), like Molly Hayward, the founder of Cora, an organic tampon subscription service and Jen Rubio, cofounder and CEO of Away, a luggage company. The thirty to forty minute co-sponsored podcasts also included interviews leading fashion and beauty influencers and thought leaders, like Jillian Mercado, a model with muscular dystrophy and modest-style fashion blogger Marwa Meme Biltagi.[56]

" In addition to paid influencers from a wide variety of backgrounds, lifestyles, and locations, as well as microinfluencers, Sephora has also taken on a multimedia approach as well, even getting in on the ever-popular podcast circuit.

Sephora on YouTube

Sephora's YouTube channel has 1.25 million followers and is a beauty-lovers treasure trove of lessons, tutorials, and tips from experts, Squad members, celebrities, and makeup and hair artists. Topics range from how to cover under-eye circles to how to perfect the best killer cat eye. While the obvious reason for being on YouTube is to sell and market products, it does so all the while educating and informing consumers and empowers them to play. But, it also seems to be great place for partnership discovery as well. Some beauty influencers have as many as thirty-two million followers. Teaming up with a beloved makeup artist or budding beauty mogul who has a built in following makes solid business sense. Huda Kattan, for example, is a makeup artist who got her start posting about her beauty and makeup routine, her favorite foundations, and how to take the perfect selfie. Today, her brand, Huda Beauty, has products in Sephora stores worldwide.

Sephora and Google

In addition to optimizing social media, onboarding influencers, and launching podcasts, Sephora found another opportunity to reach customers—through the voice-based technology like Google Home Hub. In 2018, Sephora announced its partnership with Google to "bring consumers beauty-specific commands and YouTube integrations."[57] Owners of a Google Home Hub could now request to play any of Sephora's video makeup tutorials using the Google Home without ever having to interrupt their own makeup application. Some examples of possible commands:

Hey Google, show me foundation tips videos from Sephora.
Hey Google, play everyday contour tutorial from Sephora.
Hey Google, play get ready with me eyebrow tutorial by Sephora.
Hey Google, show me bold lip color videos by Sephora.[58]

As a part of the partnership, Sephora sells the Google Home Hub in their online store and several locations. Prior to launching the Google Home Hub, Sephora had already dabbled in the voice tech space having launched one of the first Actions for Google Assistant the year prior, which allowed users to book beauty services, play quiz games, and listen to beauty podcasts. With this new Google Home Hub, customers could shop Sephora, even use the "Sephora Skincare Advisor feature to find the nearest stores, get skincare tips, and to determine their skin type."[59] Anne-Véronique Baylac of Digital for Sephora Europe and the Middle East commented, "The use of voice assistants and more recently of voice-activated loudspeakers has turned out to be more than just a fad. It's paving the way to a minor digital revolution of which Sephora wants to be a pioneer. With these first functionalities, and the collaboration with Google, we plan to test the potential and the customers' reactions to voice-assisted retailing."[60]

> " The use of voice assistants and more recently of voice-activated loudspeakers has turned out to be more than just a fad. It's paving the way to a minor digital revolution of which Sephora wants to be a pioneer. With these first functionalities, and the collaboration with Google, we plan to test the potential and the customers' reactions to voice-assisted retailing."

At the heart of Sephora's digital and innovation strategy is the customer. All the innovation, adoption of available technologies, and creation of digital and physical experiences are designed with the customer "center stage." Each product and each experience is carefully designed to make buying easy, convenient, and personal. While Sephora is largely regarded as one of the pioneers of "tech-enabled retail," it had some sharp learning curves, and outright disasters along the way, most notably recently with numerous scandals, lawsuits, and the dropping of a high-profile influencers that threatened to tarnish their seemingly "flawless" foundation.

"The worst thing a retailer or brand can do in the case of a racial bias allegation or other public relations crisis is 'to close your eyes and hope that it goes away.' More often than not, it won't."

—RONN TOROSSIAN,
president and CEO of the public relations firm 5WPR

CHAPTER FOUR

FROM THE GLAMOROUS TO THE SCANDALOUS

Though Sephora isn't known for keeping a low profile, there are some issues that they simply try to avoid altogether—to their detriment. Over the years, they found themselves in the center of several scandals. Since the early 2000s, they were involved with several lawsuits—with brand partners, consumers, celebrities, and competitors. They have also been at the center of several diversity and inclusion issues and accused of outright discrimination. As mentioned earlier, they sued Macy's in 2000 for trade dress, but while they were filing suit and battling with competitors, they had troubles brewing within their organization as well. In some cases, they were lauded for their swift response, and at other times they were met with criticism for how they responded. In all cases, there were valuable lessons learned—for Sephora and for all other retailers watching and taking notes.

" Over the years, they found themselves in the center of several scandals. Since the early 2000s, they were involved with several lawsuits—with brand partners, consumers, celebrities, and competitors. They have also been at the center of several diversity and inclusion issues and accused of outright discrimination.

Sephora Is Sued by Employees Complaining Discrimination

In 2003, five former Sephora employees who worked at a now-closed Rockefeller Center location in New York claimed that their civil rights were violated when they were prohibited from speaking Spanish. The employees went to the Equal Employment Opportunities Commission, who filed a lawsuit on their behalf. According to the *New York Times*, the women claimed they were reprimanded for speaking their native language and their supervisors "mimicked their accents and derided their culture." The former employees said if they complained about it, "they suffered even more."[1] According to one of the women, Mariela Del Rosario, "They would tell us, even on our lunch break, not to speak Spanish. . . . I understand on the floor but when I'm on my lunch break?"[2] According to Raechel Adams, a lawyer with the E.E.O.C., all of the women either quit or were fired after complaining of harassment. A spokesman for Sephora at the time told the *Times*, "Sephora does not tolerate discrimination of any kind. Furthermore, we do not have, and never have had, an 'English-only' rule in our workplace."[3]

The suit dragged on for years, but in September 2007, the case was settled "with a consent decree" though the consent decree was not on file. According to the University of Michigan Law School's Civil Rights Clearinghouse, Sephora was obligated to pay 565,000 dollars according to the settlement.[4]

Sephora is Hit with a Class Action Suit by Customers for Discrimination

One would think that a discrimination lawsuit would have changed something internally—at the very least diversity and inclusion training (which Sephora does provide). However, in 2014, another discrimination case was brought forth against Sephora. This time the plaintiffs were US citizens from Chinese descent and they were not employees, but they were VIBs and VIB Rough Members. In 2014, there was a 20 percent off sale for the top Sephora consumers. The sale was a huge hit, but unfortunately their website couldn't handle the volume and crashed. Several customers called Sephora's customer service to handle their issues, only to discover their accounts were deactivated. At the same time, Sephora made an announcement on Facebook that they blamed the site crash on the high volume of people attempting to buy in bulk at the discount prices for resale services and subsequently blocked their accounts. This, of course, coincided with the deactivations of customers with Asian names.

Shortly after, four US women of Chinese descent filed a class action suit against Sephora for what they alleged was racial discrimination. The proposed class action was filed in federal court in Manhattan and claimed that the women's accounts were deactivated simply because of their Asian surnames, and stated thousands of shoppers may have been affected.[5] According to a Reuters article, the four plaintiffs also claim they lost all of the reward points they accumulated buying hundreds of dollars of merchandise from Sephora. The women were seeking unspecified damages and a court order barring the company from engaging in the alleged practice.

According to Global Cosmetics News, in 2017, Sephora was given the go-ahead by a California federal judge to settle the class action. Sephora settled the matter and prepared to pay 950,000 dollars to those who had their accounts deactivated.[6] For their part, "Sephora vehemently denied the claims that it deactivated accounts with the Chinese domain-name email addresses at the time, claiming that consumers all over the world were affected by the 'temporary outage' of its website."[7] Then Sephora made a formal announcement stating that anyone who "as of Nov. 4, 2014, (i) had an active VIB or VIB Rouge account associated with an email address from @qq.com, @126.com or @163.com (ii) had their account deactivated on or about Nov. 6, 2014, and (iii) unsuccessfully attempted to make a purchase from the Sephora website using their Beauty Insider account at some point in November 2014 could make a claim by April 3, 2017." The estimated individual payout (depending on how many claimants) was up to 125 dollars in cash or 240 dollars in gift cards.[8]

Sephora Employee Accused of Racial Profiling and Sephora's Response

Just as the class action case was winding down in August of the same year, Sephora was hit with another PR nightmare. A viral video was making its way around the internet of a Sephora employee being accused of racially profiling customers. A Twitter user with the handle @Leek12leeek, claimed she and another woman believed they were being racially profiled, having been interrupted several times and an employee even pointed to the security guard on duty. So they confronted the Sephora employee. On her Twitter account, @Leek12leeek posted the video of her confronting the employee, who responded, "I'm from the hood." To which @Leek12leeek simply invited Twitter to "do ya thang."[9]

Sephora responded to the tweet directly apologizing and asking publicly, "We're so sorry for your store experience!" Then they asked "can you please send us a DM (Direct Message) with the exact Sephora Store you visited."

The situation seemed to be resolved. There were no further news reports about the incident, and it appears @Leeka12leeek didn't take the case further than her Twitter feed.

However, when high-profile R&B singer SZA alleged she too was a victim of racial profiling in April of 2019, things escalated quickly. According to her report to Refinery29, she used to work in the skincare department of Sephora before making it big. But during a visit to Sephora's Calabasas, California location, she believed she was profiled and accused of stealing. She, too, took her beef with Sephora to Twitter, saying: "Lmao Sandy Sephora location 614 Calabasas called security to make sure I wasn't stealing. We had a long talk. U have a blessed day Sandy."

Twitter erupted immediately, and many of her fans came to her defense. Sephora, as they say, took a minute to reply and responded the next day with "You are a part of the Sephora family, and we are committed to ensuring every member of our community feels welcome and included in our stores."[10] This time, however, it *appeared* to the public as though they took the allegations very seriously. Sephora announced they would close every single store, distribution center, and corporate office in the United States to hold inclusion workshops. In a statement announcing the closure, Sephora also announced their "We Belong to Something Beautiful "campaign," which focused on inclusion for both staff and customers. Sephora added that it "will never stop building a community where diversity is expected, self-expression is honored, all are welcomed, and you are included."[11]

A Proper Response or Planned All Along?

Though it initially *appeared* as though Sephora had taken swift action in the public eye to address the issue, according to a *Forbes* article published the day before the training was scheduled, Sephora stated it had been planning on holding these workshops long before the SZA tweet. Additionally, the "We Belong to Something Beautiful" campaign had been in development for a year, and the plan to close stores and conduct a one-hour inclusivity workshop for twenty-thousand employees had been in the works for six months as a lead-in to the campaign. The SZA incident was simply an unfortunately (or one could argue ironically) timed incident. But Sephora did acknowledge in a statement that the SZA tweet did "reinforce why belonging is now more important than ever."[12]

However, according to Joan Verdon, senior contributor to *Forbes*, announcing that the training and campaign had been planned all along and was only for one hour, not a full day, in her mind, was a major misstep. "By emphasizing that the inclusion training is part of a long-planned marketing campaign, Sephora is missing a chance to show it can pivot and take decisive action when needed to address racial bias," she writes. As a counterpoint she shared that the year prior Starbucks closed its coffee shops for a full day for training after racial profiling by an employee resulted in the arrest of two men in Philadelphia and a massive public outcry after the video went viral.

In her article, Verdon cites Katherine Milkman, a professor of operations, information and decisions at the Wharton School of Business at the University of Pennsylvania, who co-authored a research study that found diversity and inclusion training "produced mixed results."[13] Milkman's study, which measured the impact of a one-hour online training course on groups of employees, was published recently in the scientific journal *Proceedings of the National Academy of Sciences* and it found that "while the one hour of training changed attitudes, it didn't do much to change behaviors."[14] The study also concluded that "to change behavior employers might be better off devoting resources to recruiting more women and minorities for leadership roles, or change company process and policies that contribute to stereotyping and bias."[15]

Milkman gave her two-cents to Verdon about what she thought about Sephora's trainings, stating, "It's not clear these trainings target the underlying cause, and I do think that's a problem." However, she added just setting aside a time for diversity training, closing stores, and requiring employees attend does help a bit, if by only raising awareness to the employees where there once was none. "The employees need to know that this is unacceptable, that the organization takes this super seriously, and the public also needs to know that the organization takes it seriously . . . . Maybe the research doesn't support that it's going to solve the problem specifically, but it solves a different problem."[16]

> " The employees need to know that this is unacceptable, that the organization takes this super seriously, and the public also needs to know that the organization takes it seriously . . . . Maybe the research doesn't support that it's going to solve the problem specifically, but it solves a different problem."

In the same article, Verdon interviewed Ronn Torossian, president and CEO of the public relations firm 5WPR, who gave Sephora props for providing diversity training and closing the stores. "This is showing that they take these allegations very seriously and that they intend to act on them." And then adding, "The worst thing a retailer or brand can do in the case of a racial bias allegation or other public relations crisis is 'to close your eyes and hope that it goes away.' More often than not, it won't."[17]

A Possible PR Disaster

Other critics weren't as positive, stating Sephora's entire han-
dling of the event was a PR disaster and one others should
learn from. In an article for PR News called "PR Fail? Sephora
Denies Doing the Right Thing for the Right Reasons," Brooks
Wallace, an account supervisor from PR firm the Hollywood
Agency, said that Sephora missed the opportunity to show its
more "authentic and human side," adding, "In any crisis communication situation, what the public wants to hear is an apol-
ogy and admission of guilt. That humanizes a brand. It's a
signal that the brand is listening to its community, which is all
[that] the customers—and the wronged—want to hear. A simple
'we apologize, we hear you, and we're going to make it right'
would've sufficed for Sephora."[18]

Wallace continued saying that if Sephora was his client, "I'd
recommend their leadership come out with a proactive statement about how the company has learned from this experience, appreciates SZA bringing it to their attention, and
announce a yearlong effort to consistently assess diversity and
inclusion efforts—not just a one-hour workshop. Perhaps they
could even have their CEO and SZA offer a joint statement—
perhaps via a short video, if SZA were willing—about the importance of speaking up and making change happen, showing
they've made amends. Offering a little humility and eating
crow, while praising SZA for speaking up, could go a long way.
And having a top executive do it, like the CEO, would show
how seriously the company is taking it."[19]

Other PR experts in the industry concurred. "It seems like a
hollow brand message to the public to say the timing of this
training wasn't connected to this incident," added Patrick Ge-
vas, vice president of GreenRoom. "In today's challenging retail

climate, it's largely unthinkable to close all locations and miss out on sales as part of a routine. It also points to a larger issue in the training and onboarding of the employees on the front-side of hiring and taking steps throughout the year to prove their commitment to diversity. When something like this occurs, they can take swift disciplinary action and point to their track record of diversity which is ultimately a much stronger brand presence but also the right thing to do."[20]

Though they could have handled the situation better, it does show quickly and easily one employee can cause an all-out crisis for the brand, and how important hiring and ongoing training practices are. Needless to say, it's usually not "just one employee." In fact, just one day before the scheduled close for the company-wide diversity training, yet another high-profile celebrity took to Twitter and Instagram to lament Sephora employees' treatment of customers.

#NoMoreSephora

Former *Saturday Night Live* cast member, actress, and comedian Leslie Jones reported a hostile interaction between a Sephora salesperson and manager and her makeup artist, Lola Okanlawon, and her best friend's wife on June 4, 2019, in the Broadway store. Jones explained that while her friends were at the New York area Sephora store they were badly treated and left "in tears."[21] Though Sephora responded to her tweet and reaffirmed their diversity and inclusivity training that was to take place the next day, Jones believed Sephora's actions weren't sufficient. She posted again on Instagram: "I am tired of the [f–ery] yo!! If we spend money in your store we deserve customer service too. SO [F–K] YOUR STORE @sephora you got to close your store to teach your employees sensitivity how about fire they ass and hire people who got sensitivity. Cause they exist!!! I'm tired of this [s–t]!! #NOMORESEPHORA."

Sephora responded to Jones on Twitter: "@Lesdoggg we're very sorry to hear this. We have reached out via Instagram and hope to connect with you and your friends directly." The company then also gave a statement to *Us Magazine* regarding the incident: "As a company, we hold ourselves to a high, and public, set of standards around creating a welcoming space for each and every client. The information shared by Leslie Jones regarding Lola Okanlawon's experience at Sephora is concerning, and the situation she describes does not reflect our values. We have reached out to Lola to gather more information. It is our priority to build an inclusive community and a place where all clients feel respected. Our journey has not been perfect and is by no means complete. We will continue to learn and work toward this goal."

Since the launch of the campaign, Sephora has reasserted its efforts in diversity and inclusion—as seen already in the aforementioned Beauty Insider groups, its We Belong Together campaign, the announcement of twenty-four #SephoraSquad influencers with diverse backgrounds and lifestyles, and even how they talk about customers. When speaking to a Sephora employee in the Kenwood Mall in Cincinnati, who asked not to be named, she attested that Sephora is very clear about their commitment to inclusivity, and even emphasized her own effort to be considerate even with the use of gender pronouns—refraining from calling customers "she" or in the feminine third person, which was pretty standard language for years. "I try not to make any assumptions. Ever."

However, it's not just inclusion issues that plagues the store. There is an entire Reddit thread dedicated shoppers' "worst Sephora experience." Shoppers on the thread complained about rude workers who judged them on how they looked and how they dressed as well and others who were accused of shoplifting and being followed around the store by sales associates who communicate with one another and zone in on particular clients. Of course, personal experiences are just that—and they are largely anecdotal as they are on Reddit.

Woman Claims to Have Contracted an STD at Sephora and Company's Response

While the legal and PR teams at Sephora were busy with cases involving inclusivity, diversity, discrimination, and angry Reddit threads, it was hit with another unfortunate wakeup call. A claimant filed a lawsuit in 2017 alleging that she contracted the STD herpes after trying on lipstick at a Los Angeles (Hollywood and Highland) area Sephora. One of the main attractions of Sephora is of course you can sample EVERY. SINGLE. PRODUCT. before buying. Most Sephora shoppers know the etiquette. There are cotton swabs and applicators near every sample display, and absolutely no George-Costanza-level double-dipping going on. One dip and application, and then you throw out the applicator.

Sephora employees also follow rigorous protocols to maintain the samples as well. However, according to *SELF* magazine, the plaintiff claims that soon after visiting the Sephora location in 2015 where she tried on lipstick she was subsequently diagnosed with herpes on her lip by the Olive View-UCLA Medical. Herpes is incurable and can flare up at any time. The claimants, says it's a condition she "never had before this particular shopping excursion." She sued the company for, among other things, the "emotional distress" over "an incurable lifelong affliction."[22] For their part, Sephora who usually doesn't comment on litigation, came out and told *SELF* magazine "the health and safety of our clients is our foremost priority. We take product hygiene very seriously and we are dedicated to following best practices in our stores."[23]

A Quick Tutorial About Herpes

Needless to say, when word got out in 2017 of the case, it got the Sephora community talking, and even panicking. The entire Sephora experience is based on the ability to try on products and trust that the samples are clean and untainted. So just how probable is it for someone to actually contact herpes from makeup samples? According to *SELF* magazine's health reporter, "it's pretty improbable." Though, according to Tara C. Smith, Ph.D., professor of epidemiology in the College of Public Health at Ken State University and *SELF* contributor, "not totally impossible to become infected with herpes from applying a lip product."[24] Apparently, herpes can live for hours on a plastic surface and a cosmetic surface just as long, so she says, "Someone who was infected with the virus would have needed to have used the lipstick before you did." Super comforting.

> " The entire Sephora experience is based on the ability to try on products and trust that the samples are clean and untainted. So just how probable is it for someone to actually contact herpes from makeup samples?

However, according to the Centers for Disease Control, herpes can live the nerve cells and can be dormant for years before an outbreak and it's nearly impossible to know exactly when and where an infection was transmitted.[25] So even though the claimant very well may have never exhibited symptoms before trying on lipstick at Sephora, she very well could have had it in her system. Nevertheless, Sephora settled with her in the spring of 2019. No terms were disclosed, but in an official statement, Sephora stated, "We have resolved this matter while continuing to deny all of the allegations in the complaint. Sephora's entire retail concept is rooted in self-discovery and our goal is to enable an immersive environment that caters to clients' desire to learn and play uninhibited in a safe and clean environment. We take product hygiene very seriously and we are dedicated to following best practices in our stores."[26]

Even though Sephora does its best to maintain a clean and safe environment, some beauty editors advise to take precautions regardless of what stores like Sephora, Ulta, and other beauty- sample stores do. In other words: take some personal responsibility and use your own best judgment when approaching samples

▪ A DOCTOR'S ADVICE FOR SHOPPING AT SEPHORA

Dr. Joshua Zeichner, Director of Cosmetic & Clinical Research in Dermatology at Mount Sinai Hospital, advises those who shop in environments like Sephora to follow these steps to protect yourself and others:

▪ "Never apply makeup samples directly to your skin. Clean off makeup with an alcohol swab then use an applicator on the makeup and then use that to touch your skin.

- "Do not apply to open or raw skin.
- "Do not use makeup samples in stores where samples are unsupervised by employees because you don't know who has used the sample before or how it was used."[27]

Reports of contamination haven't slowed down traffic to stores like Sephora. The very reason Sephora is so successful and beloved by fans is that customers can try on almost everything in the store. Awareness isn't a bad thing though. The more educated the population is about appropriate hygiene practices the better for all involved. Awareness also pushes stores like Sephora to stay vigilant. Though from the beginning Sephora has claimed to be so, having always provided a plethora of disposable tools and cleaners throughout the store. In addition, they claim to have a highly trained staff that is assigned to various departments to assist customers with the testers and even teach those new to the testing environment.

In a 2018 statement in response to a CBC (Canadian Broadcast Company radio) report on testers, Sephora stated, "While we cannot comment on these results, as CBC has not provided full details on their findings or their collection procedures, we can say that the health and safety of our clients is our foremost priority. Not only do we have hygiene stations available for client use throughout our stores, our testers are regularly sanitized, replaced and replenished, and our associates are trained on industry hygiene standards to assist our clients. Sephora's entire retail concept is rooted in self-discovery and our goal first and foremost is to enable an immersive environment that caters to clients' desire to learn and play uninhibited. That said, we take every effort to ensure we are following best practices in our stores. We also offer many other ways for clients to test products, including guided assistance from our associates, personalized samples and digital tools that allow users to try on hundreds of products virtually."[28]

Sephora Becomes Embroiled in the Website Accessibility Litigation "Tsunami" Following as 2017 Executive Order

The legal team at Sephora had their hands full between 2017–2019, and were fighting lawsuits on various fronts. In addition to discrimination, mistreatment of customers, and being blamed for hygienic lapses, Sephora also caught the attention of American Association of People with Disabilities. According to the Americans with Disabilities Act, if a business operates for more than twenty weeks a year and has more than fifteen employees, its website is required to be accessible to those with disabilities just as a physical location is.

❝❝ In addition to discrimination, mistreatment of customers, and being blamed for hygienic lapses, Sephora also caught the attention of American Association of People with Disabilities.

How does one make a website accessible? This is a murky business and the ADA lacks clear guidelines for websites. Without clear guidelines in place and the lack of definitions, most websites haven't been able to translate requirements for physical venues into online sites—opening the doors for massive onslaught to litigation.[29] In 1999, The Web Content Accessibility Guidelines (WCAG) was published in an attempt to offer general guidelines for those with sight impairments, hearing impairments, cognitive limitations, learning disabilities, speech disabilities, photosensitivity, and limited mobility. According to Dyno Mapper, which provides site content auditing, WCAG criteria are not "technology specific" and this invites not only ambiguity, but lots of room for interpretation and hence litigation.

In 2017, a Sephora customer, Lucia Marett, claims she was attempting to close out a purchase on the Sephora and had difficulty. Legally blind, Marett attempted to use her screen-reading software but Sephora's website was not compatible with the application.[30] According to Sephora's statement at the time, their website was in line with the Web Content Accessibility Guidelines and developed by the World Wide Web Consortium. She and her lawyers, C.K. Lee and Anne Seelig of Lee Litigation Group PLLC, filed a class action lawsuit in 2017, but it was immediately dismissed "with prejudice" stating "a resolution of all matters in dispute having been made and each party to bear its own fees and costs."[31] In other words: Case closed. ("With prejudice" means it's over and the case can never be brought back to court again.) A quick Google search shows that Marett is the plaintiff in several class action suits accusing companies of similar offenses—including the Metropolitan Transportation Authority (MTA), Roche-Bobois, Red Lobster, Boston Market, Baggallini, The Clorox Company, Burt's Bees, Five Guys, Adelphi University, and even the National Association of Social Workers.

Needless to say, it seems like Sephora became the target of a litigation frenzy that followed a 2017 Presidential Executive Order for Web Accessibility. According to Garenne Bigby, for Dyno Mapper, the order would continue to "create a volatile and litigious environment, especially in the current client of regulatory uncertainty." A major implication of this order according to Bigby is that the "current tsunami of lawsuits is likely to continue," further adding "without a clear-cut set of rules to follow, website owners are largely implementing accessibility for users with disabilities (and users in general) through a means of trial and error." Bigby warned other retailers and business, "there seems very little website owners can do to protect themselves from lawsuits."[32] However, for their part, Sephora's legal team proved successful warding off further legal fees, all the while asserting their compliance.

Sephora Pulled into the College Admissions Scandal "Operation Varsity Blues" of 2018

With hardly enough time for the legal and PR teams to catch their breath, Sephora once again was pulled unwittingly into the headlines, when one of their influencers, Olivia Jade Giannulli, daughter Lori Loughlin (Aunt Becky of *Full House* fame) and fashion mogul Mossimo Giannulli, was caught up in the college admissions scandal called Operation Varsity Blues that broke in 2018. The news rocked not only the academic world, but the beauty influencer and celebrity world as well. At the time, Olivia Jade had almost two million YouTube followers, had a makeup collaboration with Sephora called the Olivia Jade x Sephora Collection Bronze & Illuminate Pallette, as well as with other top brands, like TRESemmé, Marc Jacobs Beauty, Smashbox Beauty Cosmetics, Lulus, Boohoo, and Too Faced Cosmetics. She also attended Sephora events and promoted various products on her YouTube channel and her Instagram account, where she had 1.4 million followers.

All of these collaborations came to a screeching halt when, according to court documents, Olivia Jade's parents were accused of committing fraud in an attempt to secure her admission into the University of Southern California. According to reports, the FBI alleges that Loughlin and Giannulli paid Rick Singer, a supposed admission "advisor" 500,000 dollars and even faked photoshoots so their daughters could appear as rowers, though they were never on a crew team.[33]

After the news broke, critics and angry fans were quick to point out a YouTube video Olivia Jade had made where she wasn't all that into "school" for the education, rather saying, "I do want the experience of game days, partying. I don't really care about school, as you guys all know." Soon after #boycottsephora tweets started to flood Twitter, Sephora responded quickly this time and put out a statement that Thursday announcing the end of the partnership: "After careful review of recent developments, we have made the decision to end the Sephora Collection partnership with Olivia Jade, effective immediately."[34] According to Today.com, the link to Olivia Jade's product line on Sephora's website had been "flooded with angry comments calling for Sephora to drop it after the scandal broke" and as a result, Sephora dropped the line. Sephora wasn't the only one to distance itself to Olivia Jade; TRESemmé, announced a similar statement. Even brands that did one-off sponsored programs through her and her mother distanced themselves. Hewlett-Packard asserted, "HP does not currently have a relationship with either of them."

The case isn't going anywhere anytime soon. Olivia Jade's parents were charged with several crimes including bribery. On November 1, 2019, Loughlin and her husband pleaded not guilty to the charges. The US Attorney Andrew E. Lelling alleges that Loughlin, Giannulli, and other parents "conspired to commit federal program bribery by bribing employees of the University of Southern California (USC) to gain admission for their children. In exchange for the alleged bribes, USC employees allegedly 'designated the defendant's children as athletic recruits—with little or no regard for their athletic abilities—or as members of other favored admissions categories.'"[35] In addition to pleading not guilty to bribery, Loughlin and Giannulli pleaded not guilty to money laundering, mail fraud, and honest services mail fraud. If found guilty of all, Loughlin and Giannulli could face up to fifty years for their alleged actions.

Though initially Olivia Jade took down her YouTube and Instagram accounts, she returned to Instagram and has plans to rebuild her brand, though has no plans to return to USC and Sephora has not renewed their partnership with her and has made no other public statements regarding Olivia Jade's role in the scandal. File this lesson learned under: How to Handle Situations When Influencers/Their Parents Do Dumb and Possibly Criminal Things. See also: Research the facts. Make quick game-day decision. Pull the partnerships and products. Distance yourself publicly. Never mention it again.

Sephora Carries a Product Named after Brooke Shields and Raises Some Eyebrows

In 2019, Brooke Shields filed a suit against popular makeup brand Charlotte Tilbury used her name and likeness to promote a thirty dollar pencil that enhances brows. Brooke Shields, of course, is known for several things, like nothing coming "between her and her Calvins" and of course her iconic full eyebrows. According to a complaint filed in May 2019 in a California state court, the suit file stated that the "Brooke S" shade of Tilbury's Brow Lift pencil was an attempt to "capitalize on [her] iconic eyebrows," and as a result is serving to "interfere with Shields' ability to market a cosmetics line" of her own.[36]

The complaint further asserts that "from the beginning of her career" from her days in *Vogue* and in Calvin Klein commercials to her film roles, Shields's "bold eyebrows have been the trademark of her look and a target for endorsements and collaborations" . . . and her "eyebrows have been the subject of profiles in media such as *InStyle, Elle* and *Vogue,* who even ran a story entitled, "17 Times Brooke Shields's Eyebrows Were the Best Thing in the Room."[37]

According to the suit, Tilbury "neither consulted Shields [about] nor requested permission to use" and that by naming an eyebrow product after her, it directly "interferes with Shields' ability to market such a potential collection, the unauthorized use also runs afoul of her right of publicity, which enables the actress to prevent others from commercially exploiting her name and/or likeness without permission."[38]

She says the same goes for Beautylish, Bergdorf Goodman, Bloomingdale's, JCPenney, Neiman Marcus, Nordstrom, Sephora, and Yoox Net-a-Porter, which are also named as defendants for their part in carrying and selling the product.

Shields asked the court to force the defendants to cease their use of her name and sales of the "Brooke S" products, and seeks unspecified monetary damages. Interesting also to note is that Tilbury has used celebrity names quite often in the naming of their products and haven't been met with litigation. The

"Naomi" is named after Naomi Campbell and is a brow lift in a shade for "dark brown to black" eyebrows. The "Kim KW" is named after Kim Kardashian West, the "Bosworth's Beauty" after Kate Bosworth, the "Penelope" after Penelope Cruz, the "Secret Salma" after Salma Hayek, and the "Kidman's Kiss," after Nicole Kidman. Not one of these celebrities have sued Tilbury. Shields is the first.

Neither Charlotte Tilbury nor Sephora have commented on the suit, which remains ongoing as of the writing of this book, but a representative for Shields's counsel, Alex Weingarten of Venable LLP, stated: "This is an egregious violation of Brooke's rights, which we will litigate vigorously to vindicate. Brooke Shields's career as a model, actress, author, and entrepreneur spanning decades has made Brooke (and her eyebrows) a household name."[39]

There is no word on what Sephora will or won't do. However, when searching the Sephora website for the Brooke S Brow Lift pencil, the search came up empty, though when searching simply for Charlotte Tilbury Brow Life pencil, the $30-dollar pencil does come up on the Sephora site. There is absolutely no mention of Brooke Shields anywhere. No word on whether the litigation has stopped, but it looks like Sephora is playing it safe for now.

Sephora Caught in Naming Scandals Before

Though Sephora isn't directly responsible for the original naming of the Charlotte Tilbury Brow kit, it's not the first time the retailer has suffered backlash because of the names some of their brands have decided to call the products.

Famed tattoo artist and makeup mogul Kat Von D has enjoyed a long and successful partnership with Sephora. Kat Von D first made a name for herself in her popular show *LA Ink* on the TLC network and then launched her vegan beauty line in 2008, exclusively for Sephora. The eponymous cosmetic line, which is known for its bold colors and long wear, is one of the most popular cruelty-free brands at Sephora. Kat Von D is nothing if not "colorful," and the names of her products have certainly made the headlines over the years. In 2013, Sephora immediately pulled the Kat Von D lipstick named "Celebutard" from their shelves, stating, "It has come to our attention that the name of one shade of lipstick we carry has caused offense to some of our clients and others. We are deeply sorry for that."[40] Kat Von D didn't feel the same way and took to Twitter to give some "real talk" back to her fans, tweeting and then deleting, "At the end of the day, it's just f—ing lipstick."[41]

Interestingly, Sephora and Kat Von D remained in partnership despite the temporary fallout. (Her products are still sold at Sephora and often featured as some of Sephora's bestsellers.) Sephora simply handled the dustup by 1) making a statement, 2) taking the offensively named product off their site, and 3) being more aware and mindful in the future, and responsive when similar fallouts (as in the case of the Brooke S Brow Lift) came up. Lesson learned.

Though by no means exhaustive, this list of scandals, lawsuits, and celebrity dustups in the past few years alone have showed that most of the time Sephora was responsive, took deliberate and swift action, and when warranted, immediately apologized for wrongdoing and took corrective actions to make amends wherever they could. They also proved to be quite resilient and agile when dealing with the unexpected, like the ADA website case and the college admission scandal. As a large company, with a popular name, carrying a considerable amount of high-profile brands, it's inevitable that Sephora would run into some scandals. Without minimizing the company's role in alleged cases of discrimination, it has, however, made a concerted effort to inform and train employees on diversity and inclusivity and seemed poised to be responsive in the future.

> " Though by no means exhaustive, this list of scandals, lawsuits, and celebrity dustups in the past few years alone have showed that most of the time Sephora was responsive, took deliberate and swift action, and when warranted, immediately apologized for wrongdoing and took corrective actions to make amends wherever they could.

The reality is the social, economic, and technological landscape is changing rapidly. It's not just effecting beauty retailers and the cosmetic industry, but the world as a whole. As Sephora grows and expands, it is preparing for this new and often unexpected landscape, while managing for the unexpected along the way.

"The store is where the magic happens."

—CHRISTOPHER DE LAPUENTE

CHAPTER FIVE

THE FUTURE OF HEALTH, BEAUTY, WELLNESS

With no signs of slowing down, the beauty industry is growing exponentially each year—and over half of that growth is online.[1] So what does that mean for stores like Sephora that at the heart of their brand is the experiential in-store component? Well, it means that if half is online, still *half* of all their market is still in brick and mortar establishments. Where most other retailers are downsizing and switching solely online in lieu of storefronts, the beauty industry and stores like Sephora are in the unique position of *growing* in the physical retail space. It also means it has huge potential for growth in the e-commerce market too. In fact, web sales in the beauty category outpaced the overall US e-commerce growth rate according to Internet Retailer Data.[2] This year Sephora didn't even make the Top Five of Internet Retailer's Top Growing online retailers in the beauty category. Outpacing Sephora in growth online are Glossier, Inc., (whose online sales accounted for 97.1 percent of their total sales and whose revenue grew 275 percent), Kose Corp, Harry's Inc., Ulta, and Lovely Skin.

So just how does Sephora plan on keeping up the with growth-rate of its competitors both online and in store? The best predictor of future behavior is past behavior—focusing on the customer, personalizing and customizing shopping experiences, creating an explorative and experiential journey both in-store and online, consistently rolling out new brands and partnerships, staying abreast of consumer and beauty trends, being inclusive and multigenerational, seeking out the best and newest technological trends, constantly innovating, partnering with well-known and established celebrities as well as key influencers, promoting and emphasizing an entrepreneurial spirit, and being a thought leader in the cosmetic, beauty, and wellness areas.

Most importantly, Sephora needs to keep up with the top trends shaping the future of the beauty industry, like holistic personal care, CBD-everything, inclusivity, and gender-neutral cosmetics and skin care, incorporating ancient healing and wellness practices into the modern era, partnering with female entrepreneurs, moving to event-focused and community building, and of course, big data.

Trend Spotter:
Beauty from Within—Supplements and Holistic Health Approach to Beauty

Stand in line at the grocery store and take a quick look at magazine headlines and it's easy to spot the number one growing trend in beauty—*beauty from within*. Retailers and cosmetic and skincare brands aren't just touting self-care, health, and nutrition, they are carrying and selling nutritional supplements to help their customers enhance their beauty routines. More and more people are educated and informed about how nutrition plays a role in skin and hair health, and demanding more from both their favorite beauty retailers and driving the demand for nutritional supplements. Sephora now carries supplements by Vital Proteins (collagen supplements), Hum (vitamins and minerals), and Moon Juice (supplemental powders and snacks) that promise to make customers not just beautiful, but healthy from within. Hum's cheerfully packaged supplements, according their website, are "clean, natural, triple-tested for potency and purity" and designed by Registered Dieticians. They are also "customized and personalized" based on 3-minute online nutrition profile quiz.

According to Moon Juice's website, it's not just supplement company, it's a "holistic lifestyle that goes beyond juices, milks, and snacks. It's a healing force, an etheric potion, a cosmic beacon for those seeking out beauty, wellness, and longevity." The owner and founder of Moon Juice suffered from a thyroid condition, and began eating primarily plants and had a dramatic shift in her personality, immunity, appearance, and thought. Her dramatic results inspired her to create Moon Juice, claiming on her website, "These live, medicinal foods changed me from the inside out." She is speaking the modern shopper's language, who is also looking for the next big thing that will *also change them from the inside out.*

In fact, Sephora shoppers can now fill up their carts with everything from Moon Juice's SuperHair Daily Nutrition, SuperYou Daily Stress Management, Magnesi-Om, Blue Beauty Adaptogenic Protein, and even supplement "Dusts"—Sex Dust, Brain Dust, Dream Dust, Spirit Dust, Power Dust, and Beauty Dust. In addition to partnering with brands like these, Sephora has also partnered with OLLY to create a complete line of supplements just for them. The Sephora Collection x OLLY promises everything from Skin Detox to Radiant Sleep to Lustrous Hair. Sephora customers can even find Irish Moss (a Vitamin C + E supplement) by Algenist, if they're in the market for, well, algae. As of today, Sephora carries over 116 different varieties of supplements, weight loss and management supplements, and natural herbs and botanicals.

According to WiseGuyReports.com for Reuters, "Global beauty supplements market accounted for USD 3.5 Billion in 2016 and the market is expected to reach USD 6.8 Billion by the end of 2024."[3] Furthermore, the "market is anticipated to expand at a compound annual growth rate of 8.6% over the forecast period i.e. 2016–2024."[4] Right now, geographically, the highest share in the supplements market is in Asia-Pacific, where Japan leads with the largest market, followed by China and Korea. Europe follows Asia-Pacific with more than a 25 percent share in global beauty supplements market. According to the report, "Europe beauty supplements market is majorly driven by the rising consumer concerns towards their health and their beauty appearance" whereas in North America, where it trails Europe for third place, is driven by "high disposable income and rising endorsement by celebrities."[5] What this also means, is that there is a huge market for growth in Western Markets, and we should expect to see it rise. The beauty from within trend is only just beginning here.

Trend Spotter: All Things CBD

Speaking of herbs and botanicals, Sephora's also jumped on the CBD train, another growing trend within the rising supplement and wellness trend. CBD is short for cannabidiol, a chemical compound derived from the cannabis plant that, according to Health.com, "imparts a feeling of relaxation and calm" without the psychoactive elements of THC found in pot. (Sorry to disappoint; you can't get high off of CBD.) With the rise of demand for all things CBD, beauty brands have begun to add it to their formulas. Saint Jane Beauty provides a "luxury CBD Beauty Serum" for 125 dollars. Josie Maran offers "Skin Dope" Argan Oil or "Peace, Love, & CBD" at more moderate prices. Currently, Sephora carries twenty-one brands with CBD listed as one of their main ingredients, and from the lineup of new products brands are just now releasing, that number is sure to grow as consumers demand more of it. Forget "Calgon take me away." Today's luxuriators are more like "CBD, do ya thang."

> " Currently, Sephora carries twenty-one brands with CBD listed as one of their main ingredients, and from the lineup of new products brands are just now releasing, that number is sure to grow as consumers demand more of it. Forget "Calgon take me away." Today's luxuriators are more like "CBD, do ya thang."

Cannabis: It's Not Just for Brownies Anymore

In fact, Wall Street analysts are betting on it. Jefferies analysts started seeing trends in CBD, and said online searches for "CBD beauty" increased by 370 percent within the first two months of 2019 alone.[6] Jefferies estimates that the CBD beauty segment alone could reach twenty-five billion dollars in the next ten years, and they believe that CBD will also "eat up 15 percent of the market which used to be dominated by the traditional skin-care market which currently sits at $167 billion."[7] This is quite a huge increase from what had been previously projected.

A study conducted by Brightfield Group believed the entire cannabis market (recreational, medical, and cosmetics) were supposed to be valued at twenty-two billion dollars by 2022. Jefferies, however, is predicting twenty-five billion dollars for just beauty alone and declares CBD officially mainstream. Celebrities claim using it for everything from helping them to sleep to relieving their feet from pain after a long night in high heels. Celebrities have certainly help "normalize" if not popularize the products. In 2017, CBD beauty sales were just under four million dollars in revenue, but by the end of 2018 they were seventeen million dollars.[8] For context, it's important to point out how far the traditional beauty market has transformed in just the past decade. Natural beauty products (without harsh chemicals and use only natural ingredients) are now the majority of the market.

According to Brightfield, an analytics group, in 2013 the natural beauty market accounted for 230 million dollars in sales, but in 2017, the natural beauty generated 1.3 billion dollars in annual sales. Many predict the same jumps for the CBD market. Beauty trend analysts say "natural beauty is cannibalizing traditional cosmetics."[9] Furthermore, according to Born2Invest reporter and analyst, Arturo Garcia, "If this is how the market is moving, then CBD beauty, with its natural ingredients, could only get stronger and eat up the sales of beauty products that are currently available for the mainstream crowd."[10]

Trend Spotter: Beauty Rituals Aren't Just for Women Anymore

Though from the dawn of the cosmetics and beauty industry, women have primarily been the target, men want in on the action. Gone are the days where Barbasol, Gillette, Old Spice, and Head & Shoulders had the corner market on men's personal hygiene. The field has considerably widened to include a wide variety of hair care, hair loss treatment, beard care, shaving, skincare, fragrances, supplements, and even makeup just for men. Sephora offers a wide selection of shaving kits, colognes, skin care, and what they call "grooming essentials"— like Tom Ford's seventy dollar "Fucking Fabulous Beard Oil." They also carry gender neutral lines, which can be for both male, female, or non-binary genders. On the Sephora YouTube channel, David, "The Sephora Beauty Director," wears foundation and recommends that men go into a Sephora get a Color IQ, moisture IQ to find the best foundation for them or to just "play with it" to find the best one that works for their skin and color type. (The rec goes for women too). Those in the market for gender neutral makeup can find them in the MAC, Tom Ford, Chanel, and Mark Jacobs section of Sephora.

According to Allied Market Research, men's personal care market is expected to hit 166 billion dollars in 2022, and is currently valued at 122 million dollars.[11] According to Andrew Stablein, a research analyst at Euromonitor International, "In recent years, the notion that men can't or shouldn't be using skin-care products or caring more in general about all aspects of their appearance has been receding," adding, "the average men's grooming routine isn't about just shaving, but can be aided by using skin-care products."[12]

Alison Gaither, beauty and personal care analyst at Mintel, says, "It seems that mass players are trying to expand their market and gain share in a slowing market by growing their user base."[13] She uses Sephora-sold brands like Charlotte Tilbury and Fenty Beauty as examples, who both now offer video tutorials to men who want to incorporate makeup into their self-care routine.

But, makeup is not for just men or women. According to the most recent data, the future of beauty is non-binary. Nia Warfield for the CNBC reports, "According to NPD's iGen Beauty Consumer report, nearly 40% of adults aged 18–22 have shown interest in gender-neutral beauty products. In fact, in a survey conducted by Euromonitor, more than 56% of US male respondents admitted to using some sort of facial cosmetic like foundation, concealer or BB cream at least once in 2018."[14] A reason for the increase, Larissa Jensen, a beauty industry analyst for NPD, hypothesizes is, "There are so many . . . [people] growing up with the idea that you're not tied to the gender you're born with. Beauty is no longer what you're putting out as 'ideal beauty.' Beauty can be anything, anyone, and any gender."[15]

> " But, makeup is not for just men or women. According to the most recent data, the future of beauty is non-binary.

Even up until just a few years ago, the idea of men wearing makeup was somewhat of a taboo. Manuel "Manny MUA" Gutierrez, a beauty blogger and former model for Maybelline Colossal mascara who now is the founder and CEO of Lunar Beauty, believes it was a case of misunderstanding and misinformation, saying, "I think a lot of people misconstrue a man wearing makeup as someone that is transgender or someone that wants to be a drag queen, but it's not that."[16] But Gutierrez believes times are changing, "It's all about inclusivity and encouraging people to be a little more inclusive with both men and women. I think that as time progresses and you see more men in beauty, it'll get a little bit better and better."[17]

Trend Spotter: What's Old Is New Again

Traditional medicinal and healing rituals are making a comeback—especially Ayurveda, which is becoming more mainstream. Ayurveda is a holistic approach to healing and medicine from India, and has been used for over five thousand years. It focuses on balancing, cleansing, and restoring the body, mind, and spirit, while using seasonal diets as well as prescribed eating based on one's *dosha* (or one's biological energy type—i.e., *pitta, kapha, vata*), herbal medicines, exercise, meditation, breathing, physical therapy, body brushing, massage, body oils, and cleanses. As of today, in Sephora USA there are no Ayurvedic herbal blends sold (or at least under that search criteria), but Sephora outside the US currently offer a brand called Rituals, that is based on the Ayurvedic ritual of oil cleansing, especially in Asia-Pacific and European markets. They trend has yet to become mainstream in the US, but it would be safe to expect to see such products soon.

According to Market Watch's report "Ayurvedic Market Demand, Growth, Opportunities and Analysis of Top Key Player Forecast to 2023" the global Ayurvedic market accounted for for 3,428 million dollars in 2015 and is expected to reach 9,791 million dollars by 2022, growing at a CAGR of 16.2 percent from 2015 to 2022.[18] Citing some of the reasons for the growth, the report credits some key factors, such as, "increasing demand for natural and organic products, expanding medical tourism across the globe, rising consumer awareness and growing demand for ayurvedic cosmetics products," as well as the fact that "Organic skincare products are achieving fast grip and the market is anticipated to expand even further."[19]

The report suggests that there will be "great investment opportunities" for players in the expanding global market, especially since it is predominately now in the Asia Pacific region—which take up 80 percent of the market share, leaving Europe and the US largely an untapped market area in the years to come.

Trend Spotter:
Partnering with Female Entrepreneurs and Taking a "Stand" for Social Good

Sephora is a bit ahead of the trend in this arena. In 2015, Sephora launched Accelerate, a program, which according their website, "is dedicated to building a community of innovative female founders in beauty. The six plus months-long program begins with a one-week boot camp where founders acquire the necessary skills to create a successful business." The hope is that the entrepreneurs can learn from other successful beauty mentors and entrepreneurs. At the end of the program there is a "Demo" day, in which the beauty brand founders present their companies to industry experts, venture partners, and senior Sephora leaders with the goal of future business growth, programming, and networking.

" Conrad focused her energy on an entrepreneurship program because she was concerned about the "persistent underrepresentation of female founders" in the beauty industry. Attempting to make the program both informative and fun, the program was set up much like, Conrad calls, "*Real World* meets beauty."

The first cohort started in April 2016, and included eight startups and took place in a San Francisco mansion. Corrie Conrad, who at the time was the head of Sephora's head of social impact and sustainability, launched the program after joining Sephora in 2015 (after working at Google for eight years) to help support and foster female entrepreneurship with a focus on beauty sustainability, technology, and leadership. Conrad focused her energy on an entrepreneurship program because she was concerned about the "persistent underrepresentation of female founders" in the beauty industry.[20] Attempting to make the program both informative and fun, the program was set up much like, Conrad calls, "*Real World* meets beauty." Or a more timely and apt comparison, like *Shark Tank*, one of Calvin McDonald's (Sephora USA's then CEO) "favorite shows."[21] After the weeklong boot camp, each startup returns home to continue building their companies, along with a grant from Sephora. They are then able to take advantage of online workshops and check in with their mentors, who are Sephora employees, directors, and vice presidents from all across Sephora, including outside of Sephora USA. Some of the most popular brands to come out of the first cohort are Thrive, a popular vegan and cruelty-free product, and Sahajan, a Ayurvedic Canadian brand.

After the program, startups can apply for a low-interest, "founder-friendly loan" from Sephora for more capital. According to a 2016 *Fortune* magazine article, "Sephora Accelerate's financial involvement in the companies is atypical for tech startup accelerators, which usually provide several times more than Sephora's 2,500 dollar grant, but in exchange for equity in each startup." According to Conrad, "This was not a 'What is the financial return to Sephora?' effort." As of 2019, Sephora now grants five thousand dollars per founder and typically selects ten startups to fund each year, and still takes *zero* equity in the brands.

Then why run a program that doesn't directly profit Sephora? One main reason (besides its altruistic intentions to help budding female entrepreneurs as well as the sustainability of the planet, of course) is that it helps the company stay abreast of what is coming up the pipeline and what potential brands they could distribute. Not every product, however, is selected for distribution. By early 2018, only a handful of programs have come out of Accelerate's thirty-one cohorts and have landed on the shelves of Sephora, i.e., LXMI, Vitruvi, and The 7 Virtues.

In 2019, Sephora Accelerate announced fifteen new members to the program, stating, "This talented and diverse group of female founders will receive access to the growing Accelerate alumni network—currently 31 founders strong—along with Sephora Leaders and industry experts, who will help them take the necessary steps to achieve their business objective."[22] Conrad, who is now the vice president of Sephora Stands and diversity & inclusion, stated, "We first launched Accelerate in 2016 with the goal of growing the number of female founders within the beauty industry, and to date all Accelerate participants that have aimed to land in retail have done so, including Sephora. We are proud of the community we've built so far, as we track toward our goal of supporting more than 50 women by the end of 2020. The 2019 cohort includes 15 dynamic women—our largest cohort to date—from 8 countries, including Australia for the first time. We could not be more excited to spur on their growth and to see what each can uniquely bring to the program."[23]

> **Then why run a program that doesn't directly profit Sephora? One main reason (besides its altruistic intentions to help budding female entrepreneurs as well as the sustainability of the planet, of course) is that it helps the company stay abreast of what is coming up the pipeline and what potential brands they could distribute.**

As with all of Accelerate's cohorts, the members are not just beauty or cosmetic specific. In fact, Julie Corbett, founder of

Ecologic, developed the first paper bottle made from recycled cardboard, which could possibly replace the standard plastic bottle. Concerned activists and groups have raised the warning flags about the massive amount of plastic pouring into the ocean and other ecosystems. Introducing the eco.bottle® to consumers could be a game changer not just in the plastic dependent beauty industry, but the world.

Other cohort members focused on particular ingredients. Natasha Dhayagude, the cofounder of Chinova Bioworks, developed a "a natural clean-label preservative extracted from mushrooms for the use in cosmetics and beauty industry. This ingredient is broad-spectrum against bacteria, yeast, and mold and can be customized to target individual producers' antimicrobial needs," according to Sephora Accelerate's press release.[24] Meanwhile in the area of technology, Nicole Chau, founder of La Luer, created a non-invasive at-home facial device that delivers a standard facial process that detoxes, tones, lifts, and infuses the skin with active ingredients. In the area of merchandizing, founders include Greta Fitz, who is working on a "self-care fragrance collection" that helps people "heal through the power of luxurious scent, the healing power of crystals and the setting of positive intentions."[25]

Kerrigan Behrens is the cofounder of Sagely Naturals, which infuses hemp-derived CBD into products that are natural alternatives to "traditional anti-stress, and anti-inflammatory pain relievers." Following the natural and botanical-based trend, Camille Pereira, cofounder of Médène, "offers customized essential oil blends based on a scientific algorithm to help consumers integrate oils into their daily habits as a natural solution for wellness."[26] And Patricia Camargo, cofounder of CARE Natural Beauty, is one of several all-natural and sustainable skincare lines, though her brand's products are 100 percent

Brazilian, with all locally sourced ingredients, and they use only sustainable packaging.

Other cohort members focus on hair, like Marie Cadilhac, founder of Anagem, which "supports growth for hair, lashes, brows, and beards and is composed of 95 percent natural ingredients."[27] Maeva Heim is the Australian founder of Bread Beauty Supply, a hair care company that focuses on young woman of color with "naturally curly or coily hair." Pip Summerville, also from Australia, is the founder of The Tonik, a natural supplement brand that wants to make "healthy fun, convenient, and sustainable."[28]

There are still traditional skincare brands represented but they are on the leading edge of biotech and anti-aging. Nancy Liu, the cofounder of Paektu from China, a biotech company is "aiming to provide young women with healthy and natural skincare products, using lab-cultured Cordyceps as a core ingredient. Cordyceps offer anti-aging, anti-oxidation, anti-radiation, anti-inflammatory, and detoxification results when used on the skin."[29]

In video testimonials on the Sephora website, cohort members sing the praises of Accelerate. Greta Fitz, founder of Ascention Beauty Co. says, "I want this feedback. I want them to pick things apart, because I don't want it to happen in the store." Maeva Heim, founder of Bread Beauty Supply, adds, "A lot of the big companies are run by men, and so it's super important to support women in the ecosystem and to shift the balance of power." Pip Summerville, founder of The Tonik, adds, "I'm over the moon to be a part of the whole program and take as much as I can and put it back in the business."

Jared Kassoff, an Accelerate mentor and senior manager of brand Education-Colors, believes that it is the duty and responsibility of a company like Sephora to support and encourage these women and their potentially game-changing brands. "At

Sephora we have so many amazing resources and people for these leaders to tap into, it's not just something we could do, it's really something we should do."[30]

■ HOW TO ACCELERATE

For those interested in applying to be a cohort member, the application deadline closes in the fall (typically the end of October/November) for the spring (May) cohorts, which ends with a Demo day in October the following year. Just be ready for some fierce competition and to be prepared to answer some difficult questions related to vision, innovation, products, plan, and social impact.

According to the online application, social impact is key. "Founders who go through Sephora Accelerate are expected to commit to incorporating social impact into their business mission—i.e. sourcing responsibility, adopting environmental friendly practices, or otherwise creating positive impact in their community."

Applicants are asked to submit a video telling Sephora what inspired them to start the business. (Hence, the all-important to every entrepreneur: *Why?)* They are also asked to identify a key problem they are trying to solve and why it matters. They're also asked to submit a business plan and specific plans to generate revenue, as well as ways they plan on differentiating themselves from their competitors (and who those competitors may be). Then they are asked about their ideal customer and how they will benefit from the product, and what they have learned so far about their product.

Trend Spotter: Inclusivity, Community Building, and Giving Back

Accelerate is just one of the three-pronged focuses in the Sephora Stands program which was rolled out in 2016, under the "We Belong to Something Beautiful" campaign previously mentioned. According to the Sephora Manifesto, "Sephora believes in championing all beauty, living with courage, and standing fearlessly together to celebrate our differences. We will never stop building a community where diversity is expected, self-expression is honored, all are welcomed, and you are included." Sephora Stands programs invite people to "join together to preserve our planet, support our communities, and to celebrate the beauty in each of us." With Accelerate focusing on female inclusion, leadership, and entrepreneurship as well as sustainability and social reforms, Sephora Stands Giving program was considered the "second chapter of the Belong Campaign," (the first chapter focused on gender inclusivity and was called SephoraIN). SephoraIN was created to help cultivate "positive spaces and provide resource groups and support programs for multiple employee communities. It also intended to recruit diverse and inclusive team members, and to "attract and hire employees from underrepresented communities." In addition to recruitment and support, SephoraIn also intended to educate, noting, "We understand that all of us bring unconscious bias to the workplace. SephoraIN facilitates ongoing training to develop practical strategies for inclusion, as well as host speaker series and awareness events for employees, to help "broaden their understanding on important topics."

Sephora Stands expanded their commitment to creating "a space where everyone feels like they belong" by donating one million dollars to organizations that fight for racial justice and equality across the country and create opportunities that empower underserved communities. They specifically pointed out five national organizations that they were contributing 150,000 dollars to each, including The Center for Urban Families, National CARES Mentoring Movement, National Black Justice Coalition, The National Coalition on Black Civic Participation, and the NAACP. In addition to these programs, they committed 200,000 dollars to forty-four different organizations, located in each of the forty-four retail districts throughout the US to help "fight for equality and racial justice at a local level."

Additionally, Sephora collaborated with the Values Partnership, a leading social impact agency, a council of racial justice and equality leaders to commission "a broad-based research study on the state of bias in retail, with a specific focus on the experience of people of color." The program, Sephora hopes, will "lead to recommendations that advance inclusivity and improve the retail experience for all."

> " Sephora Stands expanded their commitment to creating "a space where everyone feels like they belong" by donating one million dollars to organizations that fight for racial justice and equality across the country and create opportunities that empower underserved communities.

In addition to focusing outwardly on the community, Sephora also has an employee-assistance program, the Sephora Stands Together fund that makes it possible through gifts of time or money to provide short-term financial help to Sephora employees in times of emergency or financial hardship.

The company is also in a partnership with the Tides Foundation, a public charity and nonprofit accelerator dedicated to "building a world of shared prosperity and social justice." Sephora also provides financial support to nonprofit organizations that align with their commitment to people, planet, and community.[31]

Finally, Sephora also encourages their employees to give to causes they care about by matching dollars to the time volunteered and money given to eligible organizations. For every hour a Sephora employee volunteers at an eligible nonprofit organization, Sephora donates ten dollars to an eligible charity of his or her choice, stating on their Sephora Stands website alongside pictures of Sephora employees volunteering in the community, "Together we're making a more beautiful world."[32] One such program is Project Glimmer, an organization that inspires girls and women to believe in themselves by letting them know their community cares. Sephora has supported over 200,000 women and girls with product donations and ran programs like "Work Your Magic: A Day of Empowerment" which connects at-risk girls and women with resources that help build confidence, inner beauty, and professional skills. According to their Giving page, Sephora has assisted over 410 Sephora employees through their Together Fund, over 900 organizations with donations, and has reported that over 4,500 of their employees have donated their time or money.

In addition to charitable giving and donations, Sephora Stands has rolled out what they call "Classes for Confidence," which help to "inspire fearlessness in those facing major life transitions." Classes for Confidence are free, 90-minute hands-on beauty classes held in participating Sephora stores. Some of the in-store-only classes offered are "Brave Beauty in the Face of Cancer," and "Bold Beauty for the Transgender Community and Workforce." Since it started, Sephora has hosted over two thousand classes, reached over seventy thousand people, and according to their website, over 80 percent of the participants reported increased levels of confidence after the classes.

Trend Spotter: Sustainability

In addition to focusing on entrepreneurs who are working toward sustainability, Sephora is taking action within their own community as well, stating, "Sephora's sustainability journey is guided by the belief that together we can protect and preserve the health and beauty of our planet. We take action to cultivate sustainable practices in our retail spaces, at our headquarters, and throughout our supply chain. From environmentally responsible packaging and ingredient transparency to conscientious energy consumption, we approach every challenge as an opportunity to innovate."[33] For the past five years, Sephora has been an EPA partner, and is considered to be among the top twenty retailers in the US that procure renewable energy. It also reports having diverted 4.4 million pounds of waste from landfills in just 2018 alone.[34]

In a statement on their website, they have a three-pronged approach to sustainability—with suppliers, climate, and ecodesign. In regards to suppliers, they focus on improving workers' lives and improving product sustainability and safety, and provide a link to their detailed Chemical Policy, where they have identified a list of "high-priority chemicals for reduction and elimination." According to Sephora, "These include chemicals our clients have told us they're concerned about, plus chemicals that environmental or health groups have identified as problematic. Our goal is to see 50 percent reduction in the number of products containing these chemicals within three years. To make this change, we will partner with our current brands to find safe alternatives, support them on innovation, and advocate for more transparency in labeling."

" For the past five years, Sephora has been an EPA partner, and is considered to be among the top twenty retailers in the US that procure renewable energy. It also reports having diverted 4.4 million pounds of waste from landfills in just 2018 alone.

Sephora goes on to state that, "Our Sephora Collection products already satisfy rigorous requirements on quality, traceability, and product safety. Through our Clean at Sephora program, we're also constantly looking to bring in new brands with a more sustainable stance on chemicals." Clean at Sephora is a program that incorporates a seal (much like the famous Good Housekeeping Seal of Approval) that certifies that the products are formulated without a list of over fifty ingredients, including sulfates, parabens, phthalates, and more. Christopher de Lapuente, Sephora's CEO, states, "We aspire to be the most loved beauty community in the world, and as a part of this, Sephora has a responsibility as an industry leader to help benchmark exemplary environmental performance. New technologies, equipment, and eco-friendly materials are being introduced all the time and impact every aspect of our business—architecture, store operations, logistics, and products."[35]

In addition to certifying products, they are also concerned about the stores themselves, stating they "continue to innovate at our retail stores and distribution centers for improved energy use in an effort to reduce our greenhouse gas emissions." Ecodesign is what they call how they reduce waste in stores and from packaging—"by embracing efficient design, and encouraging the brands we carry to do the same, we save resources while incorporating recyclable materials."[36] Expect more eco-friendly and sustainable initiative, not just from Sephora and the brands they carry, but across the beauty industry.

Trend Spotter: Meeting the Customers Where They Are—Festivals, Social Media, SEPHORiA, and Home

Sephora has long been hailed as the company that meets customers where they are—and has committed to omnichannel retail experience. But, in an attempt to be more in touch with up-and-coming consumer populations, Sephora has expanded the services and store offerings to places like the music festival Coachella. Sephora was a sponsor in 2018, where it helped festival goers cool off in their air-conditioned tent, and offered free hair and makeup services. According to BuzzFeed, Hush was on hand to offer a DIY color bar, where festival goers could temporarily change their hair color or get their hair stenciled. Amika offered braiding services, and Bumble and Bumble offered "light braids" (yes, that's lights in the braids). The Sephora Collection was available for touch-ups, and there were metallic temporary tattoos. And it wouldn't be a festival without a selfie "playground," where those donning new 'dos and looks could win prizes.

In 2018, Coachella drew more than 700,000 attendees, but its influence online is why "marketers love Coachella," according to Mediakix, one of the first influencer marketing agencies. After enjoying social media success and coverage in 2018, Sephora returned in 2019 and partnered this time with popular blog The Zoe Report and created a "Zoeasis," where they set-up the "Sephora Beauty Lounge" and festivalgoers received free makeovers while hanging out with fashion, beauty, and style icon, Rachel Zoe IRL. Fans took to Instagram to post selfies of the fun. Beyond reaching millions following Coachella on social media, Sephora was also covered by *Los Angeles Magazine*, *Women's Wear Daily*, and *The Hollywood Reporter*.[37]

Coachella was also a great place for Sephora to use its own influencers as well. As mentioned previously, the #SephoraSquad regularly posts and promotes Sephora and Sephora's brands. For their part, SephoraSquad members are bit more sophisticated than most influencers. You won't find many of them standing in front of a badly-lit bathroom mirror in their selfies and tutorials. In 2016, Sephora launched an in-house content studio that offers services for photo shoots, video production, and more. According to Glossy, Sephora produced over four hundred videos in 2017, 90 percent more social media videos than the year before. The intention is to keep up with ever-shifting consumer interests, Sephora's Chief Marketing Officer Deborah Yeh told Glossy, "One of the biggest challenges is fueling the content demand for our mobile-first clients, whose social behaviors and beauty interests are constantly evolving," she said. "To stay relevant, act as a source of inspiration and a place of learning, and produce top-quality content, we must be committed to modernizing our means of staying connected to clients, partners and collaborators in an authentic way."[38]

In an attempt to connect more with clients in a meaningful way, Sephora launched a "Coachella" of their own in 2018. SEPHORiA House of Beauty is a weekend-long event that "encourages consumers to live like their favorite beauty influencers." It's described by beauty editors as a "two-day beauty bender" where they can get free samples, enjoy product previews, receive free beauty services, and take master classes with beauty experts. Elite Daily writer Stephanie Montes, said "SEPHORiA transported consumers to a beauty wonderland. Think: Willy Wonka's Chocolate factory, but for beauty." According to her "insider tips" she says, Sephora Rouge members get pre-sale ticket access. General admission is eighty dollars and each guest leaves with a "massive gift bag" filled with 250 dollars worth of products, and VIP tickets are 350 dollars, and includes a 900 dollar gift bag. A small price to pay, she says, "to upgrade our Insta feed, your beauty cabinet, and for an experience you'll never forget.[39] Besides being a hit with beauty fans, Sephora won the Digiday Content Marketing Awards for submission in the Best Experiential Marketing Campaign category for SEPHORiA.

In addition to festivals, social media, and SEPHORiA, Sephora is bringing its samples right to their customers' doorsteps. Sephora jumped on the subscription box service trend and now offers Sephora PLAY! for about ten dollars a month. The black-and-white striped Sephora box arrives monthly and includes six makeup, skincare, and haircare samples from

Sephora's top brands, five of which are trial (travel) size, and have a cash value totaling sixty-five dollars. The box also includes a reusable, recyclable makeup bag, and PLAY! book that includes tips, tricks and how-tos for each sample, as well as access to exclusive videos and tutorials. According to Sephora's website, they curate a selection of new and bestselling products and then, based a Sephora customer's PLAY! profile, they select the best version of the box to send. The service is only available in the US and only ships to the US fifty states.

> In an attempt to connect more with clients in a meaningful way, Sephora launched a "Coachella" of their own in 2018. SEPHORiA House of Beauty is a weekend-long event that "encourages consumers to live like their favorite beauty influencers."

Trend Spotter:
Continued Expansion in the Retail Space

In March 2019, Sephora announced it was expanding its footprint across the US with thirty-five new locations in 2019 alone. The first to open would be in New York's famed Hudson Yards Development, followed by ones in Palm Springs, CA; Charlotte, NC; Los Angeles, CA; Washington, D.C.; Sunrise, FL; and many more. "At Sephora, we are constantly working to further enhance, personalize and simplify the omnichannel experience for our clients, so the connection between the physical and digital is virtually seamless and highly customized at every touch-point," said Mary Beth Laughton, Executive Vice President of Omni Retail. "Clients can browse our beauty offering online or using our Sephora App, or use our digital 'Happening at Sephora' tool to discover what's happening in-store like events, classes, and services to plan their trip to their local store and even try on looks digitally with Sephora Virtual Assistant. We are thrilled to be opening in even more communities this year, bringing the best of prestige beauty, including our passionate Beauty Advisors, to more clients across the US, in real life."[40]

In the same press release, Sephora also announced that it was changing the "look" of their Beauty Advisors. They hired award-winning fashion designer and CFDA member, Nellie Partow to do so. The look was debuted for the first time at Hudson Yards. The former black and red tops worn by Beauty Advisors is now white and black, echoing Partow's and Sephora's "minimal modern luxury aesthetic."

According to the Sephora press release, the new rollout and retail concept is deeply "rooted in aesthetics, presenting its clients with the most unique product assortment, store design and client services" and in the new stores they would find "endless beauty options including 13,300 products from more than 200 carefully curated brands," ranging from cosmetics and skincare to hair care and fragrance, as well as beauty services, ranging from complimentary Makeup Minis at the Beauty Studio, a place for 20-minute one-on-one beauty sessions, from "Quick Lip" to "Lash & Dash" to "Find Your Foundation." Complimentary Skincare Minis (30 minutes each) at the Sephora Skincare Studio, such as "Mask Us Anything" to "Peel to Perfection," and "Makeup Deluxe," are where clients learn tips and techniques to recreate a custom look in a private 60-minute makeup session with an expert artist. (This is complimentary with a fifty dollar purchase.) In addition, clients can enjoy PERK Hydrating Facials, a 2-in-1 facial service that utilizes PERK technology to exfoliate, hydrate, and nourish skin for instant, glowing results. (This too is complimentary with a seventy-five dollar purchase.)

In addition to services, clients can take beauty classes, where they can learn through hands-on, interactive group tutorials. And as mentioned before, Sephora stores employee digital tools like Moisture Meter, an exclusive tool that accurately measures the amount of moisture in the skin, and various "IQ" services—Skincare IQ, Color IQ, and Fragrance IQs, which allows clients to find the best and most-personalized makeup, skincare, and perfume based on their needs and preferences. In these new locations, clients can still use the Sephora Virtual Artist during their Beauty Classes, where they can try on thousands of shades of all kinds of makeup from both third-party brands and the Sephora Collection. Clients can still also enjoy the Digital Makeover guide, which tracks all of their purchases and makes recommendations via email. Similarly, the Digital Skincare Guide sends personalized skincare regimens to clients after their skincare consultation. Sephora still used the Happening At Sephora online booking tool to make appointments or clients can use the Sephora Mobile App as well.[41]

Trend Spotter: Partnering with Luxury Treatment Centers

In 2019, Sephora also announced that it was partnering with the luxury treatment center OrangeTwist in three California locations. According to Sephora, OrangeTwist is a "fast-growing network of modern treatment shops for women and men. Created by industry leader Clint Carnell, CEO of the HydraFacial

Company, OrangeTwist is on a mission to bring the very latest in non-invasive body, face and skin treatments into the daily lives of consumers everywhere." OrangeTwist seems to be a match for Sephora, because it delivers "highly personalized experiences that help clients look and feel their absolute best." This may be the first of many partnerships.

On OrangeTwist's website, it says the partnership of the "beauty brand titans" are as "perfect a pairing as Ginger Rogers and Fred Astaire or wine and cheese." "The Sephora customer is our customer," Carnell says, noting that the trends in skin health and non-invasive aesthetic treatments are skewing younger and attracting more men, and an overall more diverse customer base. "It's pretty exciting, and we know their consumers are focusing more on skin health. They spend a lot more time on their face, and they naturally graduate to the products that we offer. Whether it's Clear + Brilliant, the Forever Young BBL, Botox or fillers, it's just a really nice, natural pull-through for their customer base."[42] The first joint locations will be in The Grove in West Los Angeles, where OrangeTwist will offer HydraFacials as well as other treatments. There are more Southern California pairings planned for 2020.

Trend Spotter: Offering Clients Credit for their Beauty and Wellness Needs

In March 2019, Sephora announced they partnered with Alliance Data to launch their first credit cards. Beginning in March, Sephora would offer Sephora Credit Card, Sephora Visa® Credit Card, and Sephora Visa Signature® Credit Card to Sephora clients. "The launch of the Sephora Credit Card exemplifies Sephora's loyalty philosophy in every sense; it considers all the most-loved aspects of Sephora—the amazing product, services, experiences and personalization—taking our client experience to the next level through special access, rewards and perks," said Sephora's Senior Vice President of CRM and Loyalty Andrea Zaretsky, "The Sephora Credit Card was the natural next step in our loyalty journey, truly adding even more value that our clients can use not only within our stores, but also in their day-to-day lives."[43]

The Sephora Credit Card and Sephora Visa Credit Card are available in select markets, and can be used at stand-alone stores and Sephora.com. Sephora cardholders can earn credit card rewards in addition to rewards in the retailer's existing Beauty Insider Program. Sephora Visa Signature cardholders also have access to further Visa Signature benefits.

Clients who apply for the credit card and are not an existing Beauty Insider member are enrolled in the program. Of course, it's important to point out, that as credit card mogul and founder of Capital One Richard Fairbank famously said, "Credit cards aren't banking—they're information."[44] All of this is to say, credit cards are important providers of data—what do people buy, when and how often do they buy, and where do they buy it. Knowing how the customer behaves is vital to understanding and creating future Sephora strategies.

Trend Spotter:
Optimizing Big Data in Beauty

Despite the previous lawsuit regarding the use of the Virtual Artist tool, Sephora is going to need to rely on big tech/big data to keep on pace with competitors, attract new customers, and curate and personalize shopping experiences based on collected consumer data. Artificial Intelligence (AI) and Augmented Reality (AR) are here to stay. Recently, ModiFace who operates Sephora's Virtual Artist, was acquired by L'Oréal, who is seen as a competitor of Sephora. Some critics argue this puts Sephora's client's data at risk, because a competitor can potentially have access to it. But, Sephora argues that with the acquisition of ModiFace, the Sephora app has seen greater engagement. Since launching the app, Sephora has seen over two hundred million shades tried on, and over 8.5 million visits to the feature, and they don't foresee the trend slowing down. "The beauty industry will likely become more and more personalized in the coming years, Parham Aarabi, CEO of Modiface said. "If you walk into a Sephora five or ten years from now, every aspect of your experience, from what you see to the products you are recommended will be customized based on your face shape, your sales history, and your preferences," Aarabi said. "That personalization will really make life easier for shoppers. But it's also better for beauty brands, because they can increase conversions by making sure their products are relevant to each shopper on a personalized level."[45]

Brian Solis, an former analyst at Altimeter, says, "Sephora is among the most advanced and advancing retailer and beauty companies that I've studied over the years. Stating the actual technology is only part of this approach, added, "Sephora is also diversifying its approach to digital transformation by focusing on the areas where other companies are struggling. Specifically, the company has studied digital customers to understand her needs and beauty and social aspirations, how she feels and shops, and more, so they adapted models, processes, and resources internally to compete with purpose." Solis also argues that Sephora recognizes that its "customers are not done evolving."[46]

Forrester analyst Brendan Witcher, commends Sephora's digitization strategies, saying "Sephora is still one of the few companies that has an actual dedicated part of their website where you can go in and personalize the experience for yourself. They are creating dialogues with customers, not monologues. And those dialogues—whether it be in store, on the app, or online—are what helps Sephora understand their customers better, and then deliver the kinds of experiences that not only meet but exceed customer expectations."[47]

Witcher says the biggest takeaway from Sephora as a case study is "to understand that your customers have pain points in their journey, and you need to solve those specific pain points."

> " Sephora is still one of the few companies that has an actual dedicated part of their website where you can go in and personalize the experience for yourself. They are creating dialogues with customers, not monologues. And those dialogues—whether it be in store, on the app, or online—are what helps Sephora understand their customers better, and then deliver the kinds of experiences that not only meet but exceed customer expectations."

Solis adds, "Executives must also empower their employees to lead digital transformation work, and escalate this work to the C-suite, so that companies can innovate instead of just respond to market trends."

Sephora's EVP of Omni Retail Mary Beth Laughton recommends to other retail companies, "Above all, remain focused on your consumer and their needs. If what you're building doesn't make their shopping experience faster or easier or more fun, it's probably not worth the investment."[48]

The Future of Beauty Retailers

Trends in beauty and wellness, merchandising, retail, technology, and data all play a pivotal role in the future success of Sephora. The beauty industry as a whole is booming, and that means more competition for Sephora. Ulta is the most obvious competitor. It's a stand-alone store—but unlike Sephora, it combines drugstore brands with prestige brands. The company's e-commerce grew more than 60 percent in 2017, and it increased its share in the prestige beauty category from less than 8 percent in 2012 to 13 percent in 2016, cutting in on Sephora's key market. According to the NPD group, the US prestige beauty industry reached 18.8 billion dollars in 2018, a 6 percent sales increase over 2017. "If I had to use one word to characterize the state of the US beauty industry today, it would be *disruption*. Whether we look at categories, brands, or retailers, there are sweeping changes taking place to the market landscape," said Larissa Jensen, executive director and beauty industry analyst at The NPD Group. "New retail concepts and technologies are changing the way we create, market, purchase, and use beauty products. Brands and retailers must not only be cognizant of these transformations and act upon them, but identify new white space opportunities to captivate consumers and further differentiate themselves from the crowd," she added.[49]

Looking out toward the future, Jensen believes, "Given the high adaptability of the beauty industry, I expect growth to continue in 2019, though it may be at a slower pace given the current economic uncertainties." Further noting, however, that she expects to "see an amplification of trends and themes that have already taken shape, including brand transparency, heightened importance of companies taking a stance on key social issues, as well as the evolution of experiential retail and pop-up concepts."[50]

As a whole, both Sephora and Ulta increased their market share from 11.8 percent to 15.4 percent between 2010 and 2017, according to Euromonitor, which predicts that they (both Ulta and Sephora) are "on the cusp of overtaking drugstores to become the second biggest channel" behind supermarkets.[51]

For all the optimistic data, however, Joel Bines, head of retail at AlixPartners, rejects the notion that beauty is "Amazon-proof." He argues, "I've been in retail for almost 30 years. It will be difficult, and I'm not saying that beauty will be the same as toilet paper. But nobody would have thought Nike would be selling on Amazon," he says. Adding, "[And as of 2017] they are." Prosper, an analytics group points out, ominously so, "Amazon is the fifth most-popular destination for cosmetics purchases."[52] So Amazon is not something prestige and specialty retailers can afford to ignore.

In a 2019 *Financial Times* article, "For Sephora, the Store is the Core to Its Beauty," Sephora global CEO Lapuente was unconcerned about Amazon's announcement in June of 2019 that it was launching its professional beauty stores aimed at the mass market. "Amazon is just another one of the many choices out there. They have a strong e-commerce offering. They don't have stores. We love that consumers love to shop online and in-store."[53] He added that that customers who buy both on- and offline tend to purchase three times more than those who buy using just one channel. "Amazon just forces us to raise our game," Lapuente argues. Where other see competition, Lapuente sees opportunity, especially in Asia, what he calls, "a fantastic opportunity" and where sales are growing 20 percent a year, and 30 percent in China. He is especially hopeful for the future, stating that Asia's younger consumers, its growing middle class, and a high interest in prestige beauty are attractive and says the region already accounts for roughly 15 percent of overall sales.[54] The pressure, Lapuente says, is "to keep on innovating" and recognizing that "Beauty is so fast-moving, you can't cruise."[55]

Looking toward the future, Lapuente is counting on innovation from both new products and the way brands reach consumers—such as voice-activated ordering like through Google and social commerce platforms like China's WeChat. But, for all of his talk of innovation, he is still counting on the consumers' desire for an experience, speaking from his bustling La Defense store, he asked the reporter for *Financial Times* looking around, "Is physical retail alive or dead?" Without waiting for answer, he responded, "It looks pretty alive to me. The store is where the magic happens."[56]

CONCLUSION

A New Era for Sephora and the Sephora Client

In January 2019, Lapuente announced a new change in command, and named Jean-André Rougeot CEO of Sephora Americas, after Calvin McDonald stepped down in July 2018 to lead Lululemon Athletica as its CEO. McDonald led Sephora through the digital revolution and implemented initiatives like the Sephora Innovation Lab, Sephora Studios, and Sephora Stands, all while expanding the company's reach. Rougeot was in many ways inheriting a strong foundation and thriving company.

Change in leadership signifies a new era for Sephora at a time of massive disruption as well as increasing competition. But if anyone is poised to take on the challenge it's Rougeot, who during his tenure at Benefit, took the company to past the billion-dollar stratosphere and helped the brand's global expansion—with the help of Sephora, of course. More than half of all Benefit sales are outside the US, and Benefit is most famous for among other things, its Brow Bar (where they offer waxing and brow filling services) in retail stores like Macy's, Ulta, and Sephora. Of course, walk through any airport, and you'll surely find a bright pink beacon of hope—the Benefit automated machine—in case you left your mascara and brow powder at home.

Lapuente was counting on Rougeot's unique and innovative approaches to prestige retail and leadership, telling WWD,

"Jean-André's extensive leadership track record, breadth of knowledge of the North American prestige beauty and retail marketplace, as well as a Sephora brand partner for more than a decade, set him up to lead our teams to continue fueling our 20 year North America success story."[1]

For his part Rougeot says, "I'm very excited to join Sephora and look forward to working with the team to build on the success of this iconic omni-retail brand. Together, we will continue strengthening Sephora's brand partnerships, innovating and delighting clients with the best experience and assortment of prestige beauty products, whether they are shopping in our stores or across our outstanding digital platforms."[2]

Rougeot's "mandate" according to WWD, will include "defending Sephora's position as the prestige beauty leader in the US and Canada, and growing the business in Mexico and Brazil."[3] Since his departure there had been speculation about who would be named to lead the next phase of the retailer's growth. A source close to the company said Rougeot "stood out as the most-qualified candidate best fit for our organization, with his long and consistent track record as a dynamic leader and in-touch, inspirational CEO and brand builder."[4]

One of the main challenges Rougeot will be facing is protecting his clients' personal information. With increased use of big data, the threat of cybercrime that affect every major retailer is real. In July 2019, Sephora announced a security breach in Hong Kong, Singapore, Thailand, Indonesia, Philippines, Malaysia, Australia, and New Zealand. Sephora stated that the customers who only used the company's online services or mobile app are affected in the incident and it didn't affect US customers. However, the exposed information included details like gender, name, surname, skin tone, ethnicity, addresses, email details, and contact details. Sephora reported that no credit card details were compromised in the incident and they have not found any misuse of the stolen data. Needless to say, such a breach creates a huge sense of distrust and worries many, who are rightly concerned that their data can be misused or abused. Protecting clients' privacy and data must be a top priority not just for Sephora, but all retailers and will continue to be a major concern in the future.

Comparison of the Generations

In addition to maintaining cyber security and keeping ahead of the competition, Rougeot faces a drastically shifting demographic, but this, of course, may work in his and the company's favor. According to a "2015 PinkReport: The Sephora Shopper" which surveyed 3,133 female beauty consumers who shop for beauty products either at Sephora stores, Sephora.com, or elsewhere, though Sephora is a magnet for women of every age group, millennials represent the largest group of dual buyers (meaning they shop in-store and online). And 69 percent of millennials say they shop in-store and online, compared to 59 percent of Gen Xers and 49 percent of boomers. Not surprisingly, boomers (76 percent) and Gen Xers (74 percent) have shopped at Sephora for at least three to ten years, with 69 percent of millennial shopping at Sephora during that time span. Millennials rank the Loyalty Program a stronger motivator than their counterparts, with 44 percent citing the Beauty Insider as "an important reason they shop Sephora."

Millennials spend the most time at Sephora, and they buy the most basic skin care products there, even if Gen Xers have the highest spending power. And according to Benchmark study, "Millennials are the most engaged in every way. Millennials have literally grown up with Sephora, most of course, not knowing a time "BS" (Before Sephora) when department stores, drug stores, and grocery stores were the only options for buying beauty. This generation also grew up with the internet practically fused to their hands. And according to the study, "It's the generation that trusts authority least, and wants proof of efficacy before she buys. She's the generation making a night of Sephora, sharing her love of Sephora on social media, and blogging about it. Capturing the hearts of Sephora millennials is crucial to success."[5]

> **Millennials have literally grown up with Sephora, most of course, not knowing a time "BS" (Before Sephora) when department stores, drug stores, and grocery stores were the only options for buying beauty. This generation also grew up with the internet practically fused to their hands.**

Another advantage Sephora has over the competition is its established retail and online presence globally. The global recognition and access makes it nearly ubiquitous, even though there are still many untapped regions and markets to explore, like the UK, Japan, South America, and of courses areas within the regions and countries where they already have a presence. There are other optimistic markers for the future of Sephora, which are also key takeaways for anyone trying to replicate or compete with Sephora. According to the study:

- Sephora is the first place consumers go to browse beauty products, according to 87 percent of women surveyed.
- The Sephora shopper finds Sephora appealing, stylish, trendy and fun, and trusts that it carries only brands and products that work.
- However, the Sephora shopper doesn't think of Sephora as "grab and go."
- The Sephora Shopper trusts the brands Sephora carries.
- The Sephora shopper loves the "made for her" feel of the shopping experience, but she doesn't want it to feel "salesy."
- In-store perks and special offers have a high rate of conversion for the Sephora shopper.[6]

Throughout all of this growth, disruption, adaptation, scandals, lessons learned and innovation though, Sephora hasn't forgotten its roots. Though it's come a long way from Limogoes and its Paris days, it's a company still focused intentionally on the customer experience—wherever they are. Though the terminology has changed as well over the years within the store setting, shopping in Sephora is still very much a theatrical experience, where customers are meant to feel enthralled while they shop, and leave feeling as glamorous as a starlet after sampling and buying the products. And to its leadership's credit, it is ever still resourceful—adapting, changing, and growing to suit the demands of a digital, fast-paced, and rapidly changing global economy—all the while trying to help its clients and employees feel like they belong to something beautiful.

BUSINESS LESSONS
AND OPPORTUNITIES

Despite its scandals and growing pains, there have been plenty of opportunities and lessons learned through Sephora's company history. They have definitely learned from their missteps and continues to apply growth strategies that positively enhance the customer experience, mainly by leveraging their successes and what already works for them. Sephora must be doing something right to have grown from a small perfume company in Limogoes, France, to a six-billion-dollar international prestige beauty retailer in the past fifty years. Below are seven quick takeaway lessons learned from Sephora:

1. Create memorable experiences. When Dominique Mandonnaud opened his small single perfume store in Limoges, France, it was virtually impossible for a customer to engage with a product. By creating a wholly new and revolutionary approach to selling cosmetics and perfume Mandonnaud put the customer's experience above all else in the selling process. As Mandonnaud's former chief designer, Chafik, said about Sephora, "When you come here, the place is enticing and a delight to the senses."[1] Though now Sephora's experiential store model as well as its full suite of events and services is being replicated by other cosmetics retailers, it also is trickling into all kinds of busi-

ness. Even banking is getting in on the experiential component of retail. Capital One now has Capital One Café's where customers can drink Peet's coffee, talk to financial advisors, and have "experiences" rather than just make banking transactions. JCPenney has even taken a page out of Sephora's playbook and is now creating more fresh experiences—beyond Sephora, of course—including styling services, a chill zone, coffee area, a selfie studio, a movement studio that offers health and wellness classes, and "Style + Substance" lifestyle workshops. Lululemon opened a flagship store in Chicago in July of 2019, that in addition to selling apparel, offers classes and workshops. It too includes a café, juice bar, lounge areas, and even tuning tables, where customers can "tune" their vibe. In a world that is going increasingly digital and where customers can buy anything they want on their phone, retailers are figuring out that customers are demanding "something more" when they are coming into a store. They want an experience—assisted self-service with highly trained and informed sales associates, the ability to sample products and try things on, all the while having fun, positive, and life-affirming experiences. In other words, customers are craving connection and they're relying on their retailers to provide that for them. If they could get what they want on their phones, then making a trip to the store has to have "something in it" for the buyer—and that something is a memorable experience.

2. Don't be afraid to seek out investors when trying to expand—but plan ahead. Mandonnaud was determined to grow and expand his brand. Though initially his first relationship with an investor/buyer Promodès failed, Mandonnaud didn't give up on his dream for expansion and

sought out other investors Apax Partners and Astorg. By getting backing of two private equity firms together, Mandonnaud was finally able to buyout his company from Promodès and execute his growth plan. But what is interesting is Mandonnaud began his relationship with his investors with his own exit in mind. He planned for his own retirement, and worked with his investors to sell the company when the time came. Both he and his investors were then incentivized to expand the company and to sell it for a profit, which they ultimately did when they sold the company to LVMH.

3. Protect Your Brand. Sephora goes to great lengths to protect their brand and image. First they do so by establishing an iconic brand image. Their iconic store fronts, interior design, and its carrying of only prestige brands immediately sets it apart from the competition. However, over the years, companies have tried to mimic the brand's look and services. Sephora didn't take it lying down and confronted those that infringed on their trade dress and won. Other ways they protect their brand image is by how they select and choose partners, social media influencers, and the brands that they care about. Everything online and on social media channels is as carefully curated as the brands inside the store. Sephora also maintains its visibility by advertising through numerous media billboards, press, radio, television, internet, mailings—and most effective is its use of target social media campaigns and their use of YouTube to create informative and entertaining tutorials that help expand their brand reach.

4. Form strategic partnerships to expand the brand. When Sephora and JCPenney announced their partnership in 2006, it turned some heads in the industry. No one was

expecting Sephora in a JCPenney. Nordstrom's maybe, Saks perhaps, but JCPenney? Not so much. Sephora wasn't afraid to take risks and saw a massive and untapped opportunity. Because JCPenney had one thousand stores throughout the country, Sephora could have access to thousands of new and potential customers, who otherwise would not have access to a standalone Sephora store. Though the store-within-a-store model is more common-place today, it was a revolutionary idea for the time. Again, more and more stores and industries are following suit—Samsung in Best Buy, Anthropologie in Nordstrom, and Finish Line, Sunglass Hut, and Starbucks in Macy's. A store-within-a-store can be a "win-win situation" for the both retailer and the tenant and provides opportunities to both enhance experiences and attract customers who are eager to learn more about a particular product or brand. And for the tenants, like Sephora, it offers them a better location than a standalone store with low risk, low overhead and minimal startup costs. Today, Sephora is located in almost 650 of JCPenney's stores across the country and in addition to its physical presence, Sephora is the exclusive online beauty product seller on JCPenney's website and now has access to millions of shoppers who head to JCPenney.com each year.

5. Create brand loyalty through promotions and programs. In the 2006 LVMH Annual Report, Sephora highlighted their "strategy of differentiation and building customer loyalty." Over the past decade the loyalty card has expanded and now boasts over ten million card holders in the US alone. It is considered to be one of the most well-known and successful rewards programs in both the retail and e-commerce loyalty communities. As a Sephora

loyalty card holder, the owner becomes what is called a "Beauty Insider." The Beauty Insider Program is Sephora's free rewards program in the United States and Canada and it lets customers earn points on all the merchandise purchases and redeem those points for rewards. Sephora has done a superb job aligning their rewards with their prestige brand. Instead of using points for a discount, Beauty Insider members can use their points to claim more beauty products at the Rewards Bazaar. Another reason why Sephora's loyalty brand is so successful is because of their personalized product recommendations, which are tailored to each customer based on their shopping history. Once again customization goes a long way in creating a positive experience for the customer and further allows them to feel connected and "a part of something beautiful."

6. Focus on omnichannel experiences. As mentioned earlier, "omnichannel" is a word to describe the cross-channel content and physical strategy that most companies or organizations employ to provide better experiences for their customers. Sephora's online channel doesn't so much as *compete* with Sephora in-store retail experience as it does help *support* the consumer experience by enhancing their ability to shop where and when it is most convenient for them. Channels can include, but are not limited to, physical locations (stand-alone stores and store-within-a-store), online, mobile apps, and even social media. Sephora had long been in on the omnichannel game. Sephora does an excellent job of integrating online and digital experiences in the retail space, and making their digital spaces feel at home and a place of connection. At the store, customers can have their face and skin analyzed

digitally to match them to the perfect foundation and makeup colors, and then have the information sent back to them so they can continue their shopping experience at home if they prefer. Back at home, while online, they can engage not only in online shopping, but groups online based on one's stored personal preferences. Everything is integrated so at the core, the customer can choose whatever experience they want, when they want, where they want it, and how they want it.

7. Invest in innovation and technology. A crucial part of Sephora's success is that they are innovative and always looking ahead to take advantage of the newest and best technologies available. They brought their web development in-house so they could be more agile and flexible and bring things to market quicker. They also could maintain the integrity of the site in-house as well—that means better images, better information about products, and ways to communicate with one another. They're also constantly evolving and creating new mobile web experiences all the time in order to stay current. Besides having an in-house team that could be agile, flexible, and work immediately to meet the needs of customers, they have integrated digital and web development into the fabric of the company and leadership. Since their company structure is customer centric, they don't silo their tech and digital departments, but rather integrate them at the highest level. They also have an Innovation Lab located in San Francisco and are always on the lookout for new brand opportunities, updates in technology, and the next big idea.

ENDNOTES

Introduction

1. Global Cosmetics Products Market Expected to reach USD 805.61 billion by 2023—Industry Size & Share Analysis. March 13, 2018. Reuters, https://www.reuters.com/brandfeatures/venture-capital/article?id=30351.

2. According to the Orbis Study referenced in the note above, "by 2050, the population over 60 years of age is expected to reach 2.09 billion. The life expectancy for women is predicted to rise from 82.8 years in 2005 to 86.3 years in 2050. Whereas for men, the expected increase for men in the corresponding period is from 78.4 to 83.6 years. Notably, the share of elderly people for cosmetic products is on rise."

3. In *Read My Lips: A Cultural History of Lipstick* by Meg Cohen Ragas and Karen Kozlowski (Chronicle Books, 1998), the authors explain how ancient Egyptian papyrus show images of women applying rouge lipstick.

4. Cosmetics and Personal Care Products in the Medicine and Science Collections. Make-up. Smithsonian Institution, https://www.si.edu/spotlight/health-hygiene-and-beauty/make-up.

5. Teresa Riordan, *Inventing Beauty: A History of the Innovations that Have Made Us Beautiful.* (New York: Broadway, 2004).

6. John Updike, "Makeup and Make-Believe: Max Factor's Life of Beautification," *The New Yorker*, August 25, 2008, https://www.newyorker.com/magazine/2008/09/01/makeup-and-make-believe.

7. Cheryl Wishover, "100 Years of Maybelline Ads Show How Little Has Changed in Beauty," Fashionista, May 12, 2015, https://fashionista.com/2015/05/maybelline-100-year-anniversary.

8. The Estée Story. Elcompaines.com, https://www.elcompanies
    .com/en/who-we-are/the-lauder-family/the-Estée-story.
9. About Us. Sephora.com. October 20, 2019.

Chapter 1

1. Sephora Holdings S.A. Cenage, Encyclopedia.com, October
    12, 2019, https://www.encyclopedia.com/books/politics-and
    -business-magazines/sephora-holdings-sa.
2. Sephora Holdings S.A. Cenage.
3. Sujata, Rao, Ritvik Carvalho, "Dashboard of a Downturn: Global
    Recession Signals," Reuters.com, June 21, 2019, https://www
    .reuters.com/article/us-global-recession-charts/dashboard-of
    -a-downturn-global-recession-signals-idUSKCN1TM1DS.
4. About Us, Boots UK, http://www.boots-uk.com/about-boots-uk/.
5. Sephora Holdings S.A, Cenage, Encyclopedia.com, October
    12, 2019, https://www.encyclopedia.com/books/politics-and
    -business-magazines/sephora-holdings-sa.
6. Bendicte Espinay, "Le groupe LVMH achete la chaine de per-
    fumeries Marie-Jeanne Godard," LesEchos.fr, May 29, 1998,
    https://www.lesechos.fr/1998/05/le-groupe-lvmh-achete-la
    -chaine-de-parfumeries-marie-jeanne-godard-793007.
7. Sephora Holdings S.A., Cenage, Encyclopedia.com, October
    12, 2019, https://www.encyclopedia.com/books/politics-and
    -business-magazines/sephora-holdings-sa.

Chapter 2

1. Julie K. L. Dam, "Looks Matter," *People*, November 8, 1999,
    https://people.com/archive/looks-matter-vol-52-no-18/.
2. Dam.
3. Dam.
4. Dam.
5. Dam.
6. Victoria Colliver, "U.S. Judge Backs Suit vs. Macy's," sfgate.com,
    February 2, 2000, https://www.sfgate.com/business/article/U-S
    -judge-backs-suit-vs-Macy-s-3076880.php.

7. Colliver.
8. Colliver.
9. Colliver.
10. "Sephora Cosmetics Co. Settles Suit," Apnews.com, June 14, 2000.
11. Julie K. L. Dam, "Looks Matter."
12. "Chafik Gasmi," Fiamitalia.it, https://www.fiamitalia.it/cn /designers/chafik-gasmi.
13. "Chafik Gasmi."
14. Julie K. L. Dam, "Looks Matter."
15. Dam.
16. Sephora Holdings S.A.
17. Sephora Holdings S.A.
18. "Jacques Levy is Appointed CEO of Sephora Europe," Business-wire.com, June 3, 2003, https://www.businesswire.com/news /home/20030603005571/en/Jacques-Levy-Appointed-CEO -Sephora-Europe.
19. "Sephora Collection," Sephora.com, https://www.sephora.com /brand/sephora-collection.
20. "NPD Reports Strong Sales of StriVectic SD, Despite Low Aware-ness; New Study Shows Women Using Stretch Mark Cream Pri-marily on Their Faces," Businesswire.com, July 19, 2004, https:// www.businesswire.com/news/home/20040719005020/en/NPD -Reports-Strong-Sales-StriVectin-SD-Awareness-New.
21. "LVMH Passionate Annual Report 2004." lvmh.fr, March 9, 2005, https://www.lvmh.fr/wp-content/uploads/2014/10/ra 2004_complet_gbr.pdf.
22. "LVMH Passionate."
23. "LVMH Passionate."
24. "J.C. Penney teams up with Sephora," Nbcnews.com, April 11, 2006, http://www.nbcnews.com/id/12270540/ns/business -us_business/t/jc-penney-teams-sephora/#.XbW7QS2ZN0u.
25. Craig Guillot, "Find Success with the Store-Within-a-Store Trend," Insights, January 12, 2018, https://insights.samsung.com /2018/01/12/find-success-with-the-store-within-a-store-trend/.
26. Guillot.
27. "J.C. Penney teams up with Sephora."
28. Craig Guillot, "Find Success with the Store-Within-a-Store Trend."

29. Katie Rosseinsky, "Sephora Sadly Won't Be Coming to the UK After All," Grazia Daily, March 6, 2019, https://graziadaily.co .uk/beauty-hair/makeup/sephora-uk-update-london/.

30. Laura Capon. "Sephora is No Longer Shipping to the UK," cosmopolitan.com, July 20, 2018, https://www.cosmopolitan.comuk /beauty-hair/makeup/a22495023/sephora-no-longer-shipping -to-the-uk-france/.

31. Capon.

32. "LVMH Passionate About Creativity Annual Report 2006," lvmh .rf, February 14, 2007, https://ddd.uab.cat/pub/infanu/30082 /iaLVMHa2006ieng.pdf.

33. LVMH Passionate.

34. LVMH Passionate.

35. LVMH Passionate.

36. Alex McEachern, "Loyalty Case Study: Sephora's Beauty Insider," July 28, 2017, https://blog.smile.io/loyalty-case-study -sephoras-beauty-insider-vib.

37. "Beauty Insider Frequently Asked Questions," Sephora.com, https://www.sephora.com/beauty/loyalty-program.

38. Alex McEachern, "Loyalty Case Study: Sephora's Beauty Insider."

39. McEachern.

40. McEachern.

41. McEachern.

Chapter 3

1. Roger C. Altman, "The Great Crash," Foreign Affairs, February 23, 2009.

2. "LVMH Passionate About Creativity: Annual Report 2008," February 5, 2009, https://www.lvmh.fr/wp-content/uploads/2014 /10/ra-lvmh-en.pdf.

3. "Jacques Levy, former CEO of Sephora died at 62," Premium Beauty News, January 4, 2012, https://www.premiumbeautynews .com/en/jacques-levy-former-ceo-of-sephora,3694.

4. Christopher de Lapuente Appointed Global President and CEO of Sephora, BusinessWire.com, March 9, 2011, https:// www.businesswire.com/news/home/20110309006073/en /Christopher-de-Lapuente-Appointed-Global-President-CEO.

5. Natalie Robehmed, "How Rihanna Created $600 Million Fortune—And Became the World's Richest Female Musician," Forbes.com, June 4, 2019, https://www.forbes.com/sites/natalie robehmed/2019/06/04/rihanna-worth-fenty-beauty/#4ed4831 f13de.

6. Pete Born, "LVMH Signs Rihanna to Create a Makeup Brand," WWD.com, April 14, 2016, https://wwd.com/beauty-industry -news/color-cosmetics/lvmh-rihanna-makeup-brand-10409670/.

7. Natalie Robehmed, "How Rihanna Created $600 Million Fortune."

8. Robehmed.

9. Robehmed.

10. Jeremy Harris, "In Conversation: Rihanna," *New York Times Style Magazine*, May 19, 2019, https://www.nytimes.com/interactive /2019/05/20/t-magazine/rihanna-fenty-louis-vuitton.html.

11. "Calvin McDonald Named President and CEO of Sephora Americas; Succeeds David Suliteanu Who Will Step Down after 13 Years to Become CEO of Kendo Brands, an LVMH Incubator of New Beauty Brands," Businesswire.com, October 24, 2013, https://www.businesswire.com/news/home/20131024006415 /en/Calvin-McDonald-Named-President-CEO-Sephora-Americas.

12. "Calvin McDonald."

13. "Calvin McDonald."

14. "Calvin McDonald."

15. Julie Bornstein, Daniel McGinn, "How Sephora Reorganized to Become a More Digital Brand," *Harvard Business Review*, June 26, 2014, https://hbr.org/2014/06/how-sephora-reorganized-to -become-a-more-digital-brand.

16. Bornstein.

17. Bornstein.

18. Bornstein.

19. Bornstein.

20. Bornstein.

21. Bornstein.

22. Bornstein.

23. Bornstein.

24. "LVMH Passionate About Creativity: Annual Report 2016," Lvmh .fr, https://r.lvmh-static.com/uploads/2017/01/lvmh_financial -documents-_va.pdf.

25. "LVMH Passionate."

26. "LVMH Passionate."

27. "Sephora Announces Innovation Lab to Usher in the Future of Retail," PRNewswire.com, March 5, 2015, https://www.prnews wire.com/news-releases/sephora-announces-innovation-lab-to -usher-in-the-future-of-retail-300046332.html.

28. "Sephora Announces."

29. "Sephora Announces."

30. "Sephora Announces."

31. "Sephora Announces."

32. "Sephora Announces."

33. "Sephora Announces."

34. "Sephora Announces."

35. "Sephora Announces."

36. "How Sephora Wins at Omnichannel," Pyments.com, March 11, 2015.

37. "How Sephora."

38. "How Sephora."

39. "How Sephora."

40. "How Sephora."

41. Priya Rao, "Sephora Head of Omnichannel Retail Mary Beth Laughton: 'We Need to Over-deliver,'" Glossy.co, December 12, 2018, https://www.glossy.co/new-face-of-beauty/sephora-head-of -omnichannel-retail-mary-beth-laughton-we-need-to-over-deliver.

42. Rao.

43. Rao.

44. Rao.

45. Bree Gonzales, "Sephora Customer Alleges Virtual Artist Kiosks Don't Inform Customers in Writing of Biometrics Collection," Cookcountyrecord.com, December 12, 2018, https:// cookcountyrecord.com/stories/511659209-sephora-customer -alleges-virtual-artist-kiosks-don-t-inform-customers-in-writing -of-biometrics-collection.

46. Gonzales.

47. Gonzales.

48. Gonzales.

49. Adam Schwartz, "New Attack on the Illinois Biometric Privacy Act," Electronic Frontier Foundation, October 4, 2018, https:// www.eff.org/deeplinks/2018/04/new-attack-illinois-biometric -privacy-act.

50. Priya Rao, "Sephora Head of Omnichannel Retail Mary Beth Laughton: 'We Need to Over-deliver.'"

51. Rao.

52. Rao.

53. Rao.

54. Elizabeth Segran, "Sephora Picks 24 Influencers for its Coveted #SephoraSquad Program," *Fast Company*, March 29, 2019, https://www.fastcompany.com/90326765/sephora-brings-25 -influencers-into-its-coveted-sephorasquad-program.

55. Segran.

56. #Lipstores, Apple Podcast Preview, https://podcasts.apple.com /us/podcast/lipstories/id1370728732.

57. Maddie Iribarren, "Sephora Brings Beauty to the Google Home Hub," Voicebot.ai, November 8, 2018, https://voicebot.ai/2018 /11/08/sephora-brings-beauty-to-the-google-home-hub/.

58. Iribarren.

59. Iribarren.

60. Iribarren.

Chapter 4

1. Susan Saulny, "Cosmetics Retailer Is Accused of Discrimination," the *New York Times*, November 8, 2003, https://www.nytimes .com/2003/11/08/nyregion/cosmetics-retailer-is-accused-of -discrimination.html.

2. Saulny.

3. Saulny.

4. Civil Rights Litigation Clearinghouse, University of Michigan Law School, April 2, 2008, https://www.clearinghouse.net/detail .php?id=8535.

5. Daniel Wiessner, "Sephora Discriminated Against Asian Customers, Law Suit Claims," Reuters.com, November 19, 2014, https:// www.reuters.com/article/us-lawsuit-sephora-idUSKCN0J31Z 020141119.

6. Georgina Caldwell, "Sephora Settles in Asian Customer Discrimination Class Action," GlobalCosmeticsNews.com, May 30, 2017, https://www.globalcosmeticsnews.com/sephora-settles-in-asian -customer-discrimination-class-action/.

7. Caldwell.

8. Ann Bucher, "Sephora Beauty Insider Class Action Settlement," TopClassActions.com, February 22, 2017, https://topclass actions.com/lawsuit-settlements/closed-settlements/496914 -sephora-beauty-insider-class-action-settlement/.

9. Cindy Diaz, "A Viral Video Shows a Sephora Employee Being Accused of Racially Profiling Customers," Insider.com, August 11, 2017, https://www.insider.com/sephora-employee-accused -of-racially-profiling-customers-2017-8.

10. Hollie Silverman, "SZA Accusation Prompts Sephora to Close All Locations Wednesday for Diversity Training," CNN.com, June 3, 2019, https://www.cnn.com/2019/06/03/business/ sephora-diversity-training/index.html.

11. Silverman.

12. Joan Verdon, "We're Closing for Diversity Training. But Not Because of The SZA Tweet," Forbes.com, June 5, 2019, https:/www .forbes.com/sites/joanverdon/2019/06/05/sephora-says-it -planned-store-closings-months-before-szas-tweet/#4dc366931d36.

13. Verdon.

14. Verdon.

15. Verdon.

16. Verdon.

17. Verdon.

18. Melissa Hoffman, "PR Fail? Sephora Denies Doing the Right Thing for the Right Reasons," Prnewsonline.com, May 6, 2019, https://www.prnewsonline.com/sephora-pr-fail.

19. Hoffman.

20. Hoffman.

21. Kiki Meola, "Leslie Jones Slams Sephora Ban After Friends Left in Tears, Challenges the Store's Inclusivity Training," UsMagazine .com, June 6, 2019, https://www.usmagazine.com/stylish/news /leslie-jones-slams-sephora-ahead-of-inclusivity-training/.

22. Amy Capetta, "A Woman Claims She Got Herpes from Sephora Lipstick." Self.com, November 3, 2017, https://www.self.com /story/woman-claims-she-got-herpes-from-sephora-lipstick -samples.

23. Capetta.

24. Capetta.

25. Abc.com Staff, "Sephora Settles Suit from Woman Who Says She Contracted Herpes from Lipstick Sample," Abc13.com, April 4,

2019, https://abc13.com/fashion/sephora-settles-suit-saying
-woman-got-herpes-from-lipstick-sample/5233541/.

26. Abc.com Staff, "Sephora Settles Suit from Woman Who Says She
    Contracted Herpes from Lipstick Sample."

27. Abc.com Staff.

28. Company Statements, "Company Responses: Makeup Testers,"
    Cbc.ca, March 16, 2018.

29. Garenne Bibgy, "Web Accessibility Lawsuits Set to Increase Un-
    der Trump," Dynomapper.com, January 25, 2018, https://
    dynomapper.com/blog/27-accessibility-testing/443-web
    -accessibility-lawsuits-set-to-increase-under-trump.

30. Paul Tassin, "Sephora Class Action Says Blind Customers Unable
    to Shop Online," Top Class Actions, February 17, 2017, https://
    topclassactions.com/lawsuit-settlements/lawsuit-news/491662
    -sephora-class-action-says-blind-customers-unable-shop-online/.

31. "Marett v. Sephora USA, Inc. New York Southern District Court,"
    Pacemonitor.com, April 11, 2017, https://www.pacermonitor
    .com/public/case/20510828/Marett_v_Sephora_USA,_Inc.

32. Garenne Bibgy, "Web Accessibility Lawsuits Set to Increase Un-
    der Trump."

33. Chloe Foussianes, "What is Olivia Jade Giannulli Doing Now?"
    TownandCountryMag.com, August 14, 2019, https://www
    .townandcountrymag.com/leisure/arts-and-culture/a28690057/.

34. Scott Stump, "Sephora Drops Partnership with Lori Loughlin's
    Daughter Olivia Jade," Today.com, March 14, 2019, https://
    www.today.com/style/lori-loughlin-s-daughter-olivia-jade-gianulli
    -loses-sephora-makeup-t150388.

35. Zack Friedman, "Lori Laughlin Pleads Not Guilty to Bribery,"
    Forbes.com, November 2, 2019.

36. "Brooke Shields Slaps Charlotte Tilbury, Sephora, Nordstrom,
    and Co. with Lawsuit Over "'Brook S.' Eyebrow Pencil," The-
    Fashionlaw.com, May 9, 2019, http://www.thefashionlaw.com
    /home/brooke-shields-slaps-charlotte-tilbury-with-lawsuit-over
    -brooke-s-eyebrow-pencil.

37. "Brooke Shields."

38. "Brooke Shields."

39. "Brooke Shields."

40. Haley Blum, "Sephora pulls Kat Von D lipstick over 'degrading'
    name," USAToday.com, November 8, 2013, https://www.usatoday

.com/story/life/people/2013/11/08/sephora-pulls-kat-von
-d-lipstick-over-offensive-name/3474443/.

41. Blum.

Chapter 5

1. Stephanie Crets, "Beauty Retailers Grow US Online Sales 24 percent," DigitalCommerc360.com, December 26, 2018, https://
www.digitalcommerce360.com/article/beauty-ecommerce
-sales/.
2. Crets.
3. Wiseguyreports.com, "Global Beauty Supplements Market 2019:
Key Players, Trends, Demand, Segmentation, Opportunities
Forecast to 2024," Reuters.com, April 15, 2019, https://www
.reuters.com/brandfeatures/venture-capital/article?id=99891.
4. "Global Beauty."
5. "Global Beauty."
6. Arturo Garcia, "CBD Beauty Industry: How Big is the Potential
Market Really?" Born2Invest, March 31, 2019, https://born2
invest.com/articles/cbd-beauty-industry-potential-market/.
7. Garcia.
8. Garcia.
9. Garcia.
10. Garcia.
11. Nia Warfield, "Men Are a Multibillion Dollar Growth Opportunity for the Beauty Industry," CNBC.com, May 18, 2019, https://
www.cnbc.com/2019/05/17/men-are-a-multibillion-dollar
-growth-opportunity-for-the-beauty-industry.html.
12. Warfield.
13. Warfield.
14. Warfield.
15. Warfield.
16. Warfield.
17. Warfield.
18. "Ayurvedic Market 2018 Global Analysis, Opportunities and
Forecast to 2023," Marketwatch.com, October 31, 2018, https://
www.marketwatch.com/press-release/ayurvedic-market-2018
-global-analysis-opportunities-and-forecast-to-2023-2018-10-31.
19. "Ayurvedic Market."

20. Kia Kokalitcheva, "How Sephora is Helping Budding Female Entrepreneurs," Fortune.com, September 9, 2016.

21. Kokalitcheva.

22. "Sephora Continues to Build a Community of Female Beauty Founders with Announcement of Fourth Sephora Accelerate Cohort," Businesswire.com, March 18, 2019, https://www.business wire.com/news/home/20190318005383/en/Sephora-Continues -Build-Community-Female-Beauty-Founders.

23. "Sephora Continues."

24. "Sephora Continues."

25. "Sephora Continues."

26. "Sephora Continues."

27. "Sephora Continues."

28. "Sephora Continues."

29. "Sephora Continues."

30. "Sephora Continues."

31. SephoraStands.com.

32. SephoraStands.com.

33. SephoraStands.com.

34. SephoraStands.com.

35. SephoraStands.com.

36. SephoraStands.com.

37. "12 Coachella 2019 Brand Activations You Can't Miss," Mediakix.com, https://mediakix.com/blog/coachella-brand-event -activations-influencers/.

38. Alexandra Mondalek, "Instagram's New Beauty-Partnerships Team Will Cater to a Growing Community," Glossy.co, May 7, 2018, https://www.glossy.co/new-face-of-beauty/instagrams-new -beauty-partnerships-team-will-cater-to-a-growing-community.

39. Stephanie Montes, "SEPHORiA House of Beauty 2019 is the Coachella of Beauty & I Got To Experience It," Elitedaily.com, October 14, 2019, https://www.elitedaily.com/p/sephoria-house -of-beauty-2019-is-the-coachella-of-beauty-i-got-to-experience -it-18754429.

40. Press Release, "Sephora Is Expanding Its Footprint Across the U.S. with 35 New Locations in 2019," Businesswire.com, March 11, 2019, https://www.businesswire.com/news/home/20190311005162 /en/Sephora-Expanding-Footprint-U.S.-35-New-Locations.

41. "Sephora is Expanding."

42. Orangetwist.com, https://orangetwist.com/sephora-orangetwist/.

43. Press Release, "Sephora Announces Launch of First Credit Card," Businesswire.com, March 14, 2019.

44. Mary Curran Hackett, *The Capital One Story*. New York: Harper-Collins Leadership, 2020.

45. Alison DeNisco Rayome, "How Sephora is Leveraging AR and AI to Transform Retail and Help Customers Buy Cosmetics," TechRepublic.com, February 15, 2018, https://www.techrepublic.com/article/how-sephora-is-leveraging-ar-and-ai-to-transform-retail-and-help-customers-buy-cosmetics/.

46. Rayome.

47. Rayome.

48. Rayome.

49. "U.S. Prestige Beauty Industry Sales Grow 6 Percent in 2018, Reports The NPD Group," NPD.Com, January 29, 2019, https://www.npd.com/wps/portal/npd/us/news/press-releases/2019/u-s--prestige-beauty-industry-sales-grow-6-percent-in-2018–reports-the-npd-group/.

50. "U.S. Prestige."

51. Anna Nicolaou and Aimee Keane, "Retail: Is the beauty industry 'Amazon-Proof'?" *Financial Times*, May 7, 2018, https://www.ft.com/content/acfe1924-4de9-11e8-8a8e-22951a2d8493.

52. Nicolaou.

53. Harriet Agnew and Hannah Copeland, "For Sephora, the Store is Core to Its Beauty," FT.com, July 25, 2019, https://www.ft.com/content/530db1bc-ae06-11e9-8030-530adfa879c2.

54. Agnew.

55. Agnew.

56. Agnew.

Conclusion

1. Jenny Fine, "Exclusive: Jean-Andre Rougeot Named CEO of Sephora Americas," WWD.com, 8 January 8, 2019, https://wwd.com/beauty-industry-news/beauty-features/sephora-ceo-jean-andre-rougeot-1202950723-1202950723/.

2. Fine.

3. Fine.
4. Fine.
5. "The Sephora Shopper (2015)," Thebenchmarkingcompany .com.
6. Denise Herich, "What is the Sephora Shopper Seeking," Gcim- agazine.com, September 20, 2015, https://www.gcimagazine .com/marketstrends/consumers/women/What-is-the-Sephora -Shopper-Seeking-328432351.html.

Business Lessons

1. Julie K. L. Dam, "Looks Matter."

INDEX

Sedgwick, Kyra, 11
Seelig, Anne, 81
Segran, Elizabeth, 60
SELF magazine, 76, 77
Sephora, viii–ix
  business history of, 1–9
  as experiential encounter, xviii–xix
  source of name, xii–xiii
Sephora Accelerate, 100–106
Sephora Americas, ix, 39–40, 125–27
Sephora Beauty Lounge, 113
Sephora Collection, xx, 18–21, 111–12
Sephora Collection x OLLY, 94
Sephora Flash, 48
"Sephora Head of Omnichannel Retail
  Mary Beth Laughton: 'We need to
  over-deliver'" (Rao), 50–51
SephoraIN, 107
Sephora Innovation Lab, 46–48, 136
"Sephora is No Longer Shipping to the
  U.K." (Capon), 26
Sephora KSA, ix
Sephora Manifesto, 107
Sephora Mobile App, 116, 117
Sephora PLAY!, 114–15
"Sephora Sadly Won't Be Coming to the
  UK After All" (Rosseinsky), 26
Sephora Skincare Studio, 116
#SephoraSquad, 60, 113
Sephora Stands, 103, 107–10
Sephora Store Companion app, 51
Sephora Studio, 27
Sephora-to-Go mobile app, 47–49
Sephora UAE, ix
Sephora Virtual Artist app, 53–54, 117
Sephora Virtual Assistant, 116
Sephora Visa® Credit Card, 118–19
Sephora Visa Signature® Credit Card,
  118–19
SEPHORiA House of Beauty, 114, 115
services, offered at Sephora, 22
"17 Times Brooke Shields's Eyebrows
  Were the Best Thing in the Room,"
  85
The 7 Virtues, 102
Shanghai, China, 22
Shanghai Jahwa United, 22
Shark Tank, 101
Shields, Brooke, 84–86

Shop 8, viii, 1–8
Singapore, 44
Singer, Rick, 83
Skincare IQ, 117
Skincare Minis, 116
skincare products
  for men, 97–98
  offered at Sephora, 21–22
Smashbox Beauty Cosmetics, xvii, 83
Smith, Tara C., 77
Snapchat, xii
social impact, 106
social media
  distributive commerce with, 57
  impact of, on beauty industry, xii
  influencers on, 59–60
social responsibility, 107–10
societal pressure, to look beautiful,
  xi–xiii
Solis, Brian, 120, 122
Souson, 13, 14
Spain, 21, 25
Spark Retention and Marketing, 29
"Square" chair, 15
Stablein, Andrew, 97–98
Staples International, 17
Starbucks, 23, 24, 55, 71, 134
store-with-a-store concept, 23–24, 134
StriVectin-SD, xx, 19–20, 27
subscription box services, 114–15
Suliteanu, David, ix, 24, 35–36
Summerville, Pip, 105
Sunglass Hut, 24, 134
Sunrise, Florida, 115
sustainability, 110–12
Switzerland, 44
SZA, 69–70, 73

technology(-ies)
  in future of beauty retailers, 120
  investing in, 136
  in sales innovations, 46–50
testers, hygiene of, 76–80
Thrive, 102
Tides Foundation, 109
TikTok, xii
TIP Workshop, ix
Tom Ford, 97
The Tonik, 105

Read on for the
Introduction from

HARPERCOLLINS
LEADERSHIP
AN IMPRINT OF HARPERCOLLINS

THE
MARVEL
STUDIOS
STORY

Available now from HarperCollins Leadership

To fully understand the success story of Marvel Studios, where should we start? Most people think of Stan Lee, the quirky old man who made cameo appearances in every Marvel Studios film up through *Avengers: Endgame*. Movie fans mourned the news of his death in 2018 at the age of ninety-five. Movie and comic book fans know he was more than just a loquacious old man; he was an inseparable part of Marvel for nearly eighty years.

Others might want to start the story with the founding of Marvel Productions in 1981, though that was really a non-event that made no significant impact on Hollywood.

How about starting with *Iron Man*, Marvel Studios' first movie made in 2008? Hardly anybody expected it to be a box office success. The concept had been kicked around in Hollywood for more than twenty years. Writers didn't want to be a part of it. The star had a rocky past. The director had never done a big superhero action film. Producers had a terrible time getting the film financed. Yet, it was a hit.

The reality is that if you really want to understand the Marvel Studios story, you need to understand Marvel Comics. And to understand Marvel Comics, you must go all the way back to how they got their start. The Marvel story starts, not with a superhero, but with a poor kid from Brooklyn in the early twentieth century, Marvel founder Martin Goodman. Much of what has made Marvel Studios and its films unique—the kinds of superheroes Marvel creates, the sheer *number* of characters in its portfolio, the way they interact in their shared universe, and the way the business evolved with the collaboration of artists and business people—was all set in motion from the very beginning. So that's where we'll begin.

Pulp Fiction before *Pulp Fiction*

Moe Goodman, who went by "Martin" most of his life, was born in 1908. His parents were from Lithuania, which was then part of the Russian Empire, and like many Jewish people during that era, they emigrated to America to seek a better life. His father, Isaac, was a tailor. His mother, Anna, raised him and his fourteen siblings.

Maybe Goodman was destined to become a publisher. According to family lore, when he was a child, he used to spend his time creating magazine mockups by cutting out stories and articles he liked and pasting them together. That was during the heyday of newspaper and magazine publishing. You couldn't walk down any street in that era without passing dozens of newsstands.

Newsstands ranged in size from tiny shacks not much bigger than a phone booth, to alcoves in the walls of a building, to long storefronts, to cigar-shop additions. Some were even sizeable stand-alone buildings with multiple open windows, where sellers stood behind narrow counters making sales. Of course, they all sold newspapers. And back in those days, a big city like New York didn't have one paper or two. It had *dozens*. In the 1920s, Brooklyn alone had five newspapers. There were papers published in the morning, papers published in the evening, and others published in Yiddish, Chinese, Japanese, and Polish. In 1900, more than 2,200 papers existed in the United States.[1]

But the big eye-catchers at the newsstands were *magazines*. They hung everywhere. The smallest stands would sell dozens of titles; the big ones could have hundreds. They plastered the walls. They hung in rows from the ceiling, creating a solid wall above the counters. They were displayed on counters and racks. Their colorful covers acted like billboards shouting to get a potential buyer's attention. And many additional magazines were sold "under the counter" since their content was deemed too risqué for open display to the public.

As Martin Goodman passed these newsstands every day on his walk to school, he would have been aware of two main magazine categories. The first were the high-end magazines such as *McClure's*, *Time*, *Harper's Weekly*, *Harper's Bazaar*, *Cosmopolitan*, and *The Saturday Evening Post*. The other kind of magazines were called *pulps*. These were cheaply produced and printed on cheap wood pulp paper, similar to newsprint. They were filled with short stories, serialized fiction, and sometimes even complete novels in genres such as westerns, horror stories, mysteries, suspense and adventure tales, and science fiction.

One thing all the pulps seemed to have in common was provocative covers. Pulp covers were usually even more colorful and attention-grabbing than those of the slick mainstream magazines. No matter what kinds of stories were inside, most covers featured either an action scene or a curvy woman, often scantily clad, in peril. In many ways, they were not unlike later comic book covers.

At their height of their popularity, more than 120 pulp titles[2] could be found every month at the 7,000 newsstands, 18,000 cigar stores, and 58,000 drugstores around the country.[3] So if you've ever wondered where movie director Quentin Tarantino got the title for his film *Pulp Fiction*, now you know.

The Goodman Method of Publishing

It's said that Goodman quit school in 1924 at age sixteen to ride the rails all over the United States before he started his career. He hopped trains, slept in hobo camps, and ate beans cooked over an open fire.

"He knew every town and it helped him to know markets," said Jerry Perles, Goodman's lawyer and friend.[4] "I don't think you could mention a town to him that he didn't know about. He is knowledgeable about this country. It helped him a great deal later on in magazine circulation."[5]

When he got back home to New York City, he took a job as a file clerk in 1929 for a company involved in the publishing world: Eastern Distributing Company.[6] Following the stock market crash, Goodman kept his job and learned the publishing business. He thrived in this environment and worked his way up the ranks, all the way to circulation manager.[7] When Eastern Distributing got overextended and filed for bankruptcy in 1932, Goodman went into business with a partner, but that relationship didn't last long. In 1934, at the age of twenty-six, Goodman became the head of his own pulp publishing business: Newsstand Publications.

Though Goodman liked magazines, he didn't focus much on their contents. He didn't set out to educate, edify, or entertain. In fact, he once told an interviewer, "Fans are not interested in quality."[8] So what was his motivation? He wanted to run a business of his own, make a good living, and take care of his family. Magazines were just the product he chose. He would provide whatever people were willing to buy.

But how did Goodman figure out what he to sell? By following trends. He watched the other magazines on newsstands that were selling well. And he constantly talked to his fellow publishers to find out what they were up to. One of his favorite strategies was to play golf with a fellow publisher. Or take a friend or rival to lunch. He would pick their brains and listen to them boast about what they were achieving. Afterward, he'd go back to his office and create a new magazine title based on the conversation. Whenever he caught wind of a bandwagon, he was lightning fast to jump on it.

For example, when Goodman observed that the Lone Ranger was popular, he created a pulp magazine called *The Masked Rider*. When Tarzan was big, he published a title called *Ka-Zar the Great*, about a boy brought up by lions (instead of apes) in the jungles of Africa. If western stories were selling, he would create a western magazine. If they were selling *really* well, he simply created more. That's how he ended up publishing nine different western pulp titles at the same time.[9] Goodman's motto could be summed up in a statement he made to *The Literary Digest* in January of 1937: "If you get a title that catches on, then add a few more, you're in for a nice profit."[10]

To minimize his financial risks, Goodman often created new companies, at least on paper, to publish some of his titles. He was soon the owner of Newsstand Publications, Western Fiction, Red Circle, and Manvis, among others. This practice enabled him to keep his taxes lower. And he could quickly shut down a company with failed titles, or protect himself from potential lawsuits. A probably unintended result was that for decades he never established a recognizable brand.

Goodman's attention was focused on two areas: the trends in the marketplace, which drove what he chose to publish, and the sale figures, which told him how each published title was doing. What happened during the time between the decision to publish a new title and a look at the sales figures from that title mattered very little to him. He relied on his editor to take care of everything in between. If Goodman expended creative energy on anything, it was on pushing his artists to create the most eye-catching covers for his magazines so that his titles would sell. And whenever he found out a title wasn't selling well enough, he'd tell the editor to kill it and create a new one.

Finally, a Comic Book

You may be wondering, *What about comic books? When did Goodman start publishing them?* That began in 1939. By then, he was making a good living cranking out magazine after magazine based on what he thought would sell. Just the previous year, he had published twenty-seven different pulp titles, with a total of *eighty-seven* individual issues.[11] One day Goodman got a visit from a friend named Frank Torpey, a salesman for a company called Funnies, Inc. Torpey pitched the idea that Goodman should branch out and publish a relatively new invention: a comic book.

Color comic strips had been around since the 1890s. In 1929, pulp fiction characters, such as Tarzan and Buck Rogers, crossed over and appeared in their own daily newspaper comic strips.[12] But it wasn't until 1935 that the first comic book was published, and just three years later, in 1938, comic books became popular with the introduction of Superman in *Action Comics #1*. The first comic book superhero, Superman, was a huge hit, selling every copy of its 200,000-print run.[13] The next year, Batman debuted in *Detective Comics #27*.

During their conversation, Torpey offered Goodman an easy inroad to publishing comic books—prepackaged illustrated content. Goodman could buy pre-made illustrated stories and simply publish them. Goodman decided to take up the offer, doing what he usually did: starting another company and inventing a new title for the magazine. This company was called Timely Comics, and the title of Goodman's first comic book was *Marvel Comics* (October issue). It soon appeared on the racks alongside newspapers and magazines.

Included in the package Goodman received from Torpey were stories with two superheroes: Namor the Sub-Mariner—half human, half Atlantean—who possessed superhuman strength, could breathe underwater, and was able to fly; and the Human Torch, an android whose origin story included his creation and eventual evolution into a crime fighter. Also included was the Angel, a costumed detective who solved crimes, and a fourth character Goodman insisted upon: Ka-Zar from his pulps.[14] Funnies, Inc. adapted an earlier Ka-Zar pulp story and created art for it.

Goodman optimistically printed 80,000 copies of this first comic book. All of them sold very quickly. So he ordered a second print run of 800,000 dated November. Incredibly, all of those sold too![15] Goodman had stumbled onto a gold mine. With the help of the Funnies, Inc. team, Goodman quickly put out a second issue (December), though he changed the name from *Marvel Comics* to *Marvel Mystery Comics*.

Continue Reading *The Marvel Studios Story*,
available now from HarperCollins Leadership

The future is within reach.

When you start making your goals a top priority, everything falls into place. Learn from the leaders inspiring millions & apply their strategies to your professional journey.

Leadership Essentials Blog

Activate 180 Podcast

Interactive E-courses

Free templates

Sign up for our free book summaries!
Inspire your next head-turning idea.
hcleadershipessentials.com/pages/book-summaries

LEADERSHIP ESSENTIALS
by HarperCollins Leadership

For more business and leadership advice and resources, visit hcleadershipessentials.com.

CPSIA information can be obtained
at www.ICGtesting.com
Printed in the USA
LVHW091918050522
717982LV00009B/188